BEST
REAL ESTATE
INVESTING
ADVICE
EVER

JOE FAIRLESS &
THEO HICKS

TABLE OF CONTENTS

BEST EVER ENDORSEMENTS

"This is a no-fluff real estate investing book that beginning and experienced investors can benefit from reading."

-Barbara Corcoran, Real Estate Mogul

"Joe is an amazing resource for the real estate industry through his writing and podcast he is giving value to industry beginners and veterans alike."

-Mark Mascia, Mascia Development, www.MasciaDev.com

"From raising money for apartments to fixing and flipping houses, this book gives investors actionable tips on how to make things happen across multiple strategies."

-Bruce Kirsch, Founder of Real Estate Financial Modeling, www.GetREFM.com

"Networking in Real Estate is so important even in this neo-world of social media. The 1990s magic report building hacks where you have a captive audience don't work and make you seem like a used car salesman. Mr. Fairless models the contemporary business mindset by giving away his best information and resources to provide others with true value. This book is a collection of these best practices to organically grow your business in the changing times."

-Lane Kawaoka, Simple Passive Cashflow, www.SimplePassiveCashflow.com

"I am currently trying to learn as much as I can about real estate investing by reading books and checking out online resources, as well as listening to various relevant podcasts. Joe Fairless provides a great resource with his podcasts. The interviews are insightful and I love the way he ask his guest the right questions. I have learned so much from listening to his podcasts. Thank you so much! Keep it up Joe!"

-J1831 (iTunes review)

"Thanks to Joe's Best Real Estate Investing Ever podcast, I was able to recently quit my job! His no fluff interviews have taught me so much. I gained the knowledge and confidence to be successful as a full time investor. I reached out to some of his best ever guest in my area (SE Michigan) who are now partners and mentors in my business! Thank you for all the actionable items you provide every day!"

-Jeff Lipple of Shelby Twp. MI, Cash For MI Home, www.CashForMIHome.com

"I ran across Joe's podcast while listening to another one and he happened to be a guest. So after I binge listened to the Best Real Estate Investing Advice Ever, I realized the amount of great value that he provides! Awesome interviews, tips, and actionable steps that I will take to be more successful. THANK YOU JOE!! Keep up the great work."

-Uz diggity (iTunes review)

"Never a day missed listening to Joe Fairless and his podcast. Was instantly hooked and the podcast quickly became my go-to source for everything real estate investing. Fast track 6 months, and closing on my first apartment deal this June! The best real estate investing advice ever for sure, and my advice, start listening today!!!"

-Giovanni Stein, Note Vestors

"Joe gets right to the point. "No fluffy stuff"! Each podcast has an incredible amount of value for the real estate investor. I have to remind myself over and over that this is a daily podcast. How does he do it?!"

-Thebiggreatriver (iTunes review)

"The 16 months of listening to your podcast, working further with you as one of your clients, and establishing new real estate connections with so many from the podcast and Best Ever Real Estate Investors have proven invaluable in moving my real estate business to a new level. Now armed with my own website, an out-of-state team that allows me to invest long distance, and a multitude of opportunities to be as active or passive as desired, I also am paying it forward utilizing the skill-sets learned from the Best Ever podcast."

-Kathy Stewart, Steward Investing, www.StewartInvesting.com

"I've been listening to "Best Real Estate Investing Advice Ever" podcast for over a year. Joe's podcast stands out because of his daily commitment of releasing a podcast. Joe covers a myriad of topics on real estate investing. You get a well-rounded podcast of all things real estate. Joe not only talks the talk, but he is an investor himself, bringing in his personal experiences that add to his overall podcast content. Daily real estate advice podcasts are hard to find, Joe does it daily with the highest quality. I truly look forward everyday to Joe's podcast. Thanks Joe for all you do!"

-Paul Santos, West USA Realty

INTRODUCTION

The carpet smelled like mildew. The walls were stained yellow. And the bed…well, I made a strategic decision not to examine that very closely because I needed my rest. Guess that's what you get when you successfully search for, literally, the cheapest hotel room in Cincinnati, Ohio.

I had a couple thousand in the bank but owed more than that. I had just gotten off a call with two investors who had previously committed to investing in my first multifamily syndication deal but were now backing out. It left a $200,000 gap and the closing date was three weeks away.

Oh yeah, my computer crashed that night too.

It was the summer of 2013 and my entrepreneurial venture wasn't going as planned.

Just six months earlier, I had held a vice president position at a New York City advertising agency. In fact, I was the youngest VP at the agency and it was a good one. I started my professional career by moving from Lubbock, Texas to New York City after graduating from Texas Tech University. I landed a job at a prestigious ad agency on Madison Avenue which also means I didn't make any money. Actually, when factoring in the hours I made less than the minimum wage for the amount of time that I worked. However, it was a good first step and I eventually went to another agency, Mr. Youth (now called MRY), where I stayed for six years and made friends for life.

But over the course of my career in advertising, I realized that I wanted to take control of my most precious resource, my time. So after I was able to save up enough money, I bought my first single-family house in Duncanville, Texas even though I lived in New York City at the time. Then I bought three more, until I reached the point in my advertising career where I was over it. Completely and entirely over it.

I read lots of real estate investing books and reached out to the authors. I learned from them, attended conferences and talked to people who were doing what I wanted to do.

Then, I left the advertising agency industry. I thought I would do career consulting and also buy apartment buildings with investors. Well, after spending $3,000 on a website and developer, I realized that I didn't have clients for career consulting so that wasn't going to work.

I quickly pivoted and put all of my attention on buying apartment communities with investors and sharing in the profits. I talked to my closest friends and got some interest, so I started looking in Tulsa, Oklahoma. I chose Tulsa because I liked the market fundamentals at the time. It was fairly close to Dallas-Fort Worth, where I grew up, and could double dip by visiting family then drive to Tulsa to visit the property. Well, it turned out that the apartment owners in Tulsa also liked the market fundamentals because I couldn't find a reasonable deal there let alone a good one for investors.

Then I came across a deal in Cincinnati, Ohio.

It was a big one: a 168-unit apartment community. I was looking at 30-unit buildings in Tulsa, but this Cincinnati deal had promise because the seller was offering a creative structure where I would take control of the property through a Master Lease. That allowed me to get into the deal with investors without the extensive approval process of the lender, since the current owner would stay on the loan until we exercised our option to purchase. I could also get into the deal for about $400,000 using this creative structure. I figured if I thought I could raise $200,000 for a 30 unit, then I could do double that for a 168-unit! Of course, I had never raised a penny before so I was not quite sure where the blissful ignorance came from. Alas, I moved forward.

And…that brings us back to this stinky old hotel room in Cincinnati.

At this point, the deal had changed and now I had to raise over $1,000,000 for the deal. There would have been zero chance of me taking on the deal, if I knew that going into it but the deal structure changed and I rolled with it. I got the brokers to put in their commission so that helped out a lot with the money we needed at closing. But getting the 1-2 punch from investors that night who had verbally committed saying I now needed to make up $200k because they were out was overwhelming – especially combined with my dwindling cash and a broke #(@$ computer.

So here's what I did.

I thought to myself "what would a billionaire do?"

Yep. That simple.

I will become a billionaire, so why not adopt the mentality of a billionaire now.

Well, a billionaire would order an appraisal then use that valuation as incentive to get more investors in the deal assuming it turned out favorably. You see, I didn't need to get an appraisal done because we weren't getting new financing. We were just taking over control of the property. Therefore, in order to save money, I hadn't ordered one because those things can cost a couple of thousand dollars.

I immediately called an appraiser and we got a valuation of $6,700,000 which was $350,000 more than the option price I negotiated ($6,350,000). I then brought that appraisal back to my current investors and one of them covered the $200,000 gap.

Oh, I also got my computer fixed.

Now I control over $56,000,000 of real estate. I've got a daily real estate investing podcast called the Best Real Estate Investing Advice Ever Show, which is the world's longest running daily real estate podcast. I'm very proud of how far I've come in three years since starting real estate full-time.

Why do I tell you this story?

Because it's real. It's an actual story from an actual investor. And, my friend, that's what this book is all about.

Actual stories. From actual investors. Learning from people who are actively investing in real estate, or closely connected to real estate investing.

We've handpicked some of the best episodes from my first 100 podcast episodes and put them in this book. Plus, we've added action items to help you implement the advice. After all, what does advice without action give you? Nothing.

Enjoy the stories and hope you learn as much as I did from them.

Joe

PART ONE:

THE BEST BUY-AND-HOLD INVESTING ADVICE EVER

CHAPTER 1: LEARN THE REAL STORY BEHIND A PROPERTY

"The difference between a successful person and others is not a lack of strength, a lack of knowledge, but rather a lack of will" – *Vince Lombardi*

Best Ever Guest: Justin Bajema

Justin Bajema is the founder of Access Property Management Group in Grand Rapids, Michigan. He is also an active investor focusing on multifamily properties and deal syndication.

Episode 13

http://accesspmgroup.com

After Justin graduated from high school, the whole academic game was not engaging or challenging enough for him, so he went directly into the workforce. Justin quickly grew bored with the 9-5 grind and believed there had to be something more to life than what he was seeing around him. Justin found his calling in May 2001, when he made the choice to join the Marines. When speaking with the Marine recruiter, he made it clear that the he would join as long as they promised to give him an infantry position. A couple months later, the 9/11 attacks occurred, so his life was about to change forever. Having demanded to be in the infantry, Justin knew that he would be sent to war, so he learned early on to be careful what you wish for. The four years and two tours that Justin served as a Marine provided him with a very interesting and unique experience. Reflecting on this time, he says he would never give it back but he would never want to do it again either.

The beginning stages of Justin's real estate career occurred when he got back from his first tour in Iraq. He received a care package containing a book that changed his life forever, "Rich Dad, Poor Dad" by Robert Kiyosaki. This was the spark for his entrepreneur, investing, and real estate love. Justin says it was probably the first book he had ever read front to back. It changed everything for him. He started reading hundreds of books, and listening and reading everything he could get his hands on.

During Justin's second tour, he was injured severely on two occasions, and was blown up on a third. After the third injury, he was immediately Medevac'd out of the country, and spent six weeks in the hospital. Due to his injuries, he required eight surgeries on his legs and had to learn how to walk again. Justin quickly became fed up with being in the hospital because it was very depressing being around people that were hurt, injured, and wounded. He knew that he had to go out and do something with his second chance at life. It was like a calling, saying "there is no way I made it through this stuff and not do something." Six months later, Justin ran a 25k to prove to himself that he could do something after being blown up and learning how to walk again.

Using what he learned from his newfound love for real estate and after getting a second chance at life, Justin started investing in single-family homes after the market crashed. He believes it was pure luck that he happened to get into real estate at the same time as the global economic meltdown. Justin focused on purchasing small, single-family foreclosures, fixing them up, and renting them out. He continued to follow this model, but he eventually realized that buying at the right price was just one aspect of a great deal. The other aspect is property management. The Marines Corps takes pride in commitment, courage, honor, and professionalism. However, Justin was not really seeing this in the real estate industry. What he did see were amateur, mom & pop property management companies that were lazy and were not leveraging technology or many of other things that were out there. Starting from almost nothing, with only $105 in his bank account and zero clients, Justin started his own property management company. Six and a half years later, he manages over $40 million in assets.

Transition from SFR to Apartments

While Justin was working on expanding his property management company, he also continued to grow his single-family rental portfolio. When his company was managing over 300 units, he decided to give multifamily investing a try. Justin's first experience with multifamily was when he syndicated a small student housing complex by raising 100% of the $2.05 million purchase price from investors he had built relationships with during his property management career.

Student housing is a totally different animal compared to conventional multifamily. However, it was an incredible learning experience for Justin. He identified the property as an under-utilized asset because of deferred maintenance and poor management, repositioned the property, and put it under his management company, resulting in a great first multifamily deal. Justin believes that if he never learned how to manage properties well, he would have never identified this opportunity.

Invest In Yourself

Justin believes it is important to invest in yourself before you invest in a deal. He understands that many people want to skip the learning period and just get a deal done. The reality is, however, that you will get your education one-way or the other. Justin is not saying that you should only read real estate books and never take any action. You should be learning, growing, and executing at the same time. He knows from first-hand
실행

experience the importance of investing in yourself first. If Justin had never taken the time to read "Rich Dad, Poor Dad" cover to cover, he may have never gotten started. In addition, without the expertise that he gained through starting and running a property management company, he would have never met the individuals who invested in his student housing deal and he would have not been able to identify the value-added opportunity in the first place.

Advice in Action #1: Make sure that you are taking the time to invest in yourself before and while you grow your real estate business. Below is a list of resources Justin has and continues to utilize to invest in himself:

- **Podcasts**
- **Books**
- **E-books**
- **Audiobooks**
- **Conferences and seminars**

The Internet is also a great source for education! There are so many real estate related forums, blogs, and news articles out there, so you have many options to choose from.

The key is consistency. Justin loves to learn and is growth driven, so he is never going to stop educating himself. The world in general is changing rapidly. If you look back in history, there are many examples of companies that were around for over a hundred years. However, they didn't keep up with what was happening in the marketplace and ended up going out of business or being purchased. If you are not constantly learning and evolving, it could be game over.

Advice in Action #2: Justin formed a habit of reading every morning. If you find yourself making the excuse of not having enough time to read, commit to waking up 10 minutes early and using that extra 10 minutes to read in the morning. I personally read one book a month

and have applied lessons I've learned from those books in my real estate business.

The Numbers Tell the Story

"The numbers tell the story" seems basic and elementary, but Justin believes this is the key to the whole real estate game. It is very important to be able to understand what the numbers are telling you. The types of questions Justin asks about a property in order to make sure he has an understanding of the whole picture are:

- *What are the trends?*
- *What type of real estate are the majority of people investing in?*
- *Is the property at its peak performance?*
- *How is the property operating?*

Advice in Action #3: Having a negative answer to one or more of these questions does not automatically mean it is a bad deal, but you need to be really careful and make sure that you understand what you are trying to do. To reiterate again, if you do not invest in yourself first, you will not even understand how to read these things when analyzing a deal, and you will truly be at a disadvantage.

As a value-add investor, Justin looks for properties that are mismanaged so he can go in and add value to the tenants, community, building, investors, and themselves as managers. Many people are just looking at the profit, but he believes the secret is adding value and reaping the profits that result from that added value. Justin wants to identify situations where it is a win-win all-round. Justin does not believe in the cliché that "there is always a winner and a loser," because through firsthand experience, he knows it is possible to added value to not only himself, but the tenants, his investors, the building, and the longevity of the asset as well.

Justin has seen many examples of investors who did not let the numbers tell the story, and the negative consequences that followed. He was looking at the pro forma (property's financial projections) for an apartment complex and discovered that there wasn't any money going towards maintenance or CapEx (CapEx stands for capital expenditures which is money saved up and then spent on things that benefit the property over a long period of time i.e. roof, HVAC, parking lot, etc.). They were ignoring these numbers in order to prop up the properties net operating income (NOI), which in turn, inflated the value of the property. For apartment complexes, you derive the property's value using the NOI and the local cap rate (NOI/cap rate = property value), so the higher the NOI, the higher the property value. Another issue was that the current owners were not screening tenants properly. They were more worried about filling leases any way they could in order to get a higher NOI.

Early in his investment career, Justin learned from his mentors that you do not buy based off of the pro forma. In a pro forma, you will find higher income projections and lower expense projections. However, these numbers are not how the property is currently operating. Justin is not going to pay for improvements he is going to have to perform. It is great that the pro forma shows the property can potentially produce an extra $100,000 in value, but he is not going to pay for what it can "do." He is going to pay for what it did do.

Advice in Action #4: Do not buy based off of the pro forma alone. If you do, you are more than likely overpaying, so make sure you are purchasing based on a property's historical financials.

When Justin is looking at a property, he wants to see a minimum of the last three years of the actual financials, but ideally, the last five years. By looking at the last three to five years of financials, he can see if the property's NOI is trending up or down, which paints a picture of the property's operations. Unless owners are really on top of things, they are typically not repositioning the property five years in advance, but rather three years, two years, one year or maybe not at all.

Advice in Action #5: When you are purchasing investment properties, it is important to analyze the historical financials, but it is even more important to have a one, two, three, etc. year business plan on what you are going to do after you purchase the property:

- **What value-added opportunities have you identified?**
- **When will you perform these value-added tasks?**
- **How much will the property's value increase as a result of these value-added tasks?**
- **What is your exit strategy?**

These are the types of questions you need to be aware of and have answered before moving forward.

The NOI is only one part of the property's story. Justin also asks to see the profit/loss or balance cash flow statement. By looking at this information, he can see where they are putting their money and identify any potential large capital improvements that have been put off.

Advice in Action #6: You need to be a true investigator when looking at the numbers. Commit to taking hard stances based on your investment qualification criteria, like requiring at least 3 years of historical financials.

In the next chapter, you will get three pieces of Best Ever Advice on:

1. Why you should never sell a property…period
2. A step-by-step approach for using market data to perform due diligence
3. How to hone your psychology and create massive success

CHAPTER 2: LEVERAGING YOUR REAL ESTATE ASSET WITHOUT SELLING IT

"If you don't go after what you want, you'll never have it. If you don't ask, the answer is always no. If you don't step forward, you are always in the same place" – Nora Roberts

Best Ever Guest: J. Massey

J. Massey invests in both residential and commercial real estate. He has amassed a portfolio of over 300 properties in the last 6 years.

Episode 14

http://www.CashFlowDiary.com

Before getting started in real estate, J. Massey was in one of the worst spots of his life. He was in a place he could never imagine that was full of struggle and overwhelming challenge. His wife was pregnant at the time and had a medical condition called hyperemesis that made it nearly impossible for her to eat or drink. Life was stressful to say the least. One day, to blow off steam, J. joined some friends to play volleyball.

During the game, he landed on another player and punctured a lung. Because he also has asthma the injury made it impossible for him to walk and talk simultaneously. A self-employed financial planner, J. could no longer perform his duties and was forced to make a tough choice. He quickly learned that "if you don't work, you don't eat."

Dominos started to fall. First J. couldn't work, then he couldn't feed his family, and then his primary residence was foreclosed. His family and he were squatting in a bank-owned property; his cars were repossessed and his electricity was turned off. Times were dire for the Massey family.

Around this time, a friend approached him and said, "J., you should become a real estate investor." Staring at his friend, he thought how could he be a real estate investor when he had no money and was, in fact, selling his personal possessions on eBay to eat?

Still, J. knew his situation couldn't get any worse, so he listened to his friend's advice. The rest is history. Today J. is the founder and CEO of www.CashFlowDiary.com and specializes in deals that require none of his personal cash or credit. He uses private capital from investors and provides them with turnkey real estate solutions, including apartment buildings and commercial properties. He educates others on the processes and systems he has developed in the area of raising private capital, a topic on which he speaks and writes frequently.

J. learned that if a "need" is strong enough anything is possible. He believes that no one has a money problem. Instead, they have an idea problem. As he explains it, if you let someone else's ideas come into your life and you begin to take action on those ideas, anything can happen for you.

By taking action on the idea from his friend, J. went from the worst spot of his life to owning more than 300 residential and commercial properties!

Never Sell. Period.

J.'s Best-Ever advice is to never sell… period. It may seem like a good business decision at the time you sell a property, but looking back you will wish you never had. J. says he regrets selling any of his properties, and that the best method to build wealth is to keep the property in your portfolio and learn how to continually leverage the equity time and time again. If you can do this successfully and do your proper due diligence, you can be in a position to leverage more and more equity over time. This is how you build a real estate empire.

An example of leveraging equity would be taking a SFR that is owned free and clear and having a private investor or bank give you a loan against the property. This is one of many different ways to leverage equity, but all of them are derivatives of this one simple approach. For example, in 2014, J. was working with a vacant commercial building. He did some TI (tenant improvements), which increased the property's value and, in turn, the improvements increased the equity. After putting a tenant in place, J. sold a portion of the equity to investors, took the cash and repeated the same process.

Advice in Action #1: As your portfolio grows and you amass more and more equity, it is important to have the right financial team in place. We are not all built to look at everything the same way, so have a solid team of financial experts who can help you find creative, efficient ways to manage your equity to the fullest.

Using Data for Due Diligence

J. created a 4-step process that uses data from reisreports.com, which consolidates market and submarket research data on apartment, office, retail, industrial and self-storage property types to perform due diligence on the properties and ensure that his real estate investing team members are performing their duties as agreed:

1. *Look up "rent per square foot" on reisreports.com*

2. *Calculate market rent*

3. *Ask the property manager what they believe the per-unit rent should be*

4.   *Ask them why they believe the amount they estimate is what the per-unit rent should be*

For example, let's say J. is looking at 1,000-square-foot rental property. Reisreports.com states that the "rent per square foot" in the area is $0.60, so the property should rent for $600 (1,000 square feet x $0.60 per square foot). J. calls the property manager to ask what they believe the unit will rent for and they say $800. Since this is not the same information he obtained, J. then asks the property manager "why" they think it will rent for $800. If they have actionable true information about the marketplace, they should be able to defend the $800 rental value.

At this point, depending on how the property manager responds to the "why" question, J. can decide whether or not to hire them. Since he already has accurate rental rate information, he also has something by which to gauge the answer.

- If the property manager doesn't know, lies, or makes up a number, is this someone worth hiring?

- If they have the opposite answer, like the example above, can they back it up with credible information?

- Even if they state the same rate, it is still important to see if they can back it up with credible information.

- Ideally, the property manager should have and be able to share further information, which is a sign of a professional who is active in the market and knows what they are doing.

Advice in Action #2: The main points of the due diligence process are to confirm with cautious suspicion, to test someone's character, and make sure they are providing accurate information. Use this process to make an educated decision on whether or not you should hire them. This due diligence process can be applied when screening any potential team member, not just property managers and property management companies.

Honing Your Psychology for Success

J. believes the difference between someone who is successful and someone who is not, has a lot to do with how one measures success. He finds that unsuccessful people typically measure incorrect things. As entrepreneurs, we are in control of the game, but a lot of times we make the game too difficult on ourselves.

People feel unsuccessful, which is a feeling brought on by setting the line of success very high. In short, they feel bad about not having gotten to their success goals yet. Had they set more realistic expectations, they would not feel unsuccessful.

If you tell yourself that "I am will be successful when I do a real estate deal" the converse is also true: "If I haven't done a deal yet, then I am unsuccessful."

J. says if you were to lower the bar for success and instead say, "I am successful because I remembered to brush my teeth today," you would have a greater feeling of being successful. While this may seem silly at the surface, it makes a lot of sense. By achieving small goals you start to build up more and more positive momentum until you find yourself saying, "Of course. I will write an offer today, of course I will raise $100,000 today!"

As J. puts it, you don't even realize you are successful many times throughout the day. For example, if you are headed to an appointment, you were successful by getting in the car on time, starting the car and making it to the appointment. All of these little successes are key to the greater feelings of accomplishment and will help you build the positive momentum you need to achieve your higher goals in real estate investing.

Advice in Action #3: Every morning for the next week, take out a journal and finish the following sentence:

- **Five reasons I am successful today are...**

After a week, you will have 35 reasons why you are successful. On a day during which you are having a hard time, go back and read these reasons. By doing so, it is impossible to not feel good about yourself!

J. also believes that it is important to manage your life in 15-minute intervals. He literally sets an alarm on his phone for every 15 minutes. When the alarm goes off, he asks himself "in the last 15 minutes, did I move forward or away from my goal? "

Follow his lead. In the worst-case scenario, you'll only waste 15 minutes and then you will be back on track. To fully grasp the power of time management, J. says that in a week, there are 7 days and you only need to win 4 of them. In a month, there are 4 weeks and you only need to win 3 of them. In a year, there are 12 months and you only need to win 7 of them. That means you can goof off 5 months of the year and still be good.

Advice in Action #4: Try managing your life in 15-minute intervals for a day and see how you feel at the end of it. This can easily be done using the alarm app on your cell phone. What do you have to lose? You may find it was the best success habit you've ever used!

In the next chapter, you will get three pieces of Best Ever Advice on:

1. Why it's important to set up roots when beginning to invest in a new market

2. Why you can't rely on a property's financials and what you better know in order to run the numbers properly

3. A step-by-step process on how to manage expectations with contractors

CHAPTER 3: THE IMPORTANCE OF A SOLID TEAM, UNDERSTANDING OPERATIONS, AND MANAGING EXPECTATIONS

"Everyone has a plan until they get punched in the face." – Mike Tyson

Best Ever Guest: Chris Winterhalter

Chris Winterhalter is the co-founder and managing member of KGC Partners, an investment group that focuses on the multifamily and hotel segment. Chris is currently focused on the multifamily side, specifically in the Cincinnati, Ohio market.

Episode 17

http://www.kgcpartners.com

Chris got his start in real estate at the end of 2008. After graduating with a degree in Operations Management, he moved to California and took a position as an Inventory Manager at a 3rd party logistics firm. Chris had an entrepreneurial mindset growing up, so he always knew he wanted to invest in real estate. His initial intentions were to invest in California while continuing to work full-time and spend all of his time outside of work researching and learning more about real estate. After a year of working full-time and researching, his goals evolved, and he decided to invest outside of California. The main reason for this evolution was due to a California investor he connected with who was investing in

St. Louis, Missouri. Chris built a solid team in the St. Louis market, invested in multi-families, and eventually moved to St. Louis in order to take his business to the next level.

After meeting his current business partner, who had over 10 years of experience in hotel construction projects, Chris entered the hotel space. He and his partner have completed 9 major hotel construction projects totaling over 1,500 guest rooms. They also own 119 multi-family units together with no other outside investors. Chris currently resides in Chicago, which is 4-5 hours from the St. Louis market, as well as his hometown and new target market, Cincinnati, Ohio. Having experience in multiple hotel construction projects and multi-family rentals, Chris has accumulated a vast amount of invaluable knowledge, specifically in regards to the importance of building a solid team, understanding the full operations process, and managing expectations with contractors.

Building a Solid Team

In hindsight, Chris says he would have invested in the Cincinnati market instead of selecting St. Louis. After being in St. Louis for about a year, he actually wanted to make a change and start investing in Cincinnati because of the similarities between the two markets, like the diversity of employers, and both being Midwestern cities, among other metrics. The reason that Chris was unable to make this change was because he had already spent a lot of time building a solid team in St. Louis. He believes that "once you start to set roots in a place, it's difficult to gain traction in another market without doing the same things."

Setting up roots in a market is very important. The market location strongly influences the type of projects available and the type of team members you can find and attract. The more good relationships you create, and the more you establish a track record as someone who closes deals, the more opportunities you will be presented with. You are going to find that the majority of the opportunities you receive will come through these types of relationships, so the stronger the team members you have, the better the opportunities.

Understanding Financials vs. Understanding the Operations

Chris's best real estate investing advice ever is "financials are only as good as the person writing them." Financials, in general, are subject to considerable manipulation, but especially in real estate. Income producing properties fall into this category, with apartment buildings having the most manipulations. Within the apartment building category, the smaller deals (typically under 50 units, but 50-100 units as well) are the worst in regards to incorrect financials. For example, Chris found two properties that were on the same street, had similar looks, price per unit, unit mix, and rents. One was a 10-unit property advertised at a 15% cap rate and the other was a 120-unit property advertised at a 10% cap rate. Why is it that the 10-unit was more efficient than the 120-unit? Chris discovered that in reality, this was not the case. It was due to the person who put the numbers together.

When getting started in real estate, the hardest part is evaluating deals. This is because beginners do not fully understand what it takes to actually operate a property properly. The finance and mathematics portion are important, but it will not mean anything unless you understand the entire operations process behind these numbers. Chris strongly urges newer investors to start by getting a basic understanding of the entire real estate process, including operations, acquisitions, dispositions, management, and rehab. At that point, you can use the knowledge to look at the financials and recognize which parts make sense and which are incorrect, and then you can change the financials or run your own numbers to evaluate the deal.

Chris also stresses the importance of understanding the ins and outs of how property management companies operate. Even if you decide to outsource your property management, you really need to understand the process if you want to be a successful investor. You can have them help you underwrite the deal, but realize that it will be your asset, not theirs. They will be managing the property for you, but at the end of the day, they are in the business of making a profit for not only you, but also for themselves. If you do not understand the process and instead, just rely on the judgment of the property management company, your investment can go downhill fast or you will find that you will not get the returns you were expecting from the underwriting process. This is why there are many large owner operators who are property management companies, because they know that no one is going to treat their asset better and give it more attention than them!

Advice in Action #1: When getting started in real estate, begin with a small SFR (single family residence) or duplex and manage the property yourself for at least a year. This is a simple way to get hands on property management experience.

After getting a basic understanding of all aspects of the real estate process, you can decide which piece of the puzzle you like the most, master it, and make that a part of what your responsibilities are for your deals moving forward.

Advice in Action #2: The following are best practices that Chris has used in order to learn the entire real estate process:

- **Interning or working within a real estate organization**

- **Self-managing your first investment**

- **Asking to work alongside a property manager, contractor, broker, or other real estate professional. Either proactively seek out these individuals or spend time with them during the process of you deals.**

Commit to at least one of these best practices above. You will pick up many of the operations by observing and actively participating. Remember to focus on all aspects of the real estate process. If you

decide to work alongside a property manager one week, select a contractor the next week, a broker the week after that, and so on.

Managing Expectations with Contractors

When Chris first started off, he contracted out everything. He is very detailed oriented, so he was able to stay on top of all the contractors by having numerous checks and balances in place and relying on written contracts. Chris quickly realized these relationships with the contractors were not always black and white. Having everything in writing is a must, but the most important thing you need to do is manage expectations realistically.

Understand that in every relationship, there are two-sides to the coin with two different perspectives. Just because you believe you have portrayed your expectations sufficiently or have everything written in the contract does not mean that your contractor is on the same page. Chris makes sure that he communicates up front as much as he can by walking, visualizing, detailing, and managing not only his expectations, but the contractor's as well. By neglecting to do so, he would be setting up the project for failure.

Advice in Action #3: In order for you to fully grasp the importance of managing expectations, next time you have an issue with your contractor, or with anyone else, ask yourself the following question:

- **Did I communicate all of the project expectations up front and in detail or did I assume that we were on the same page?"**

If you are truly honest with yourself, you will realize that this issue, as well as the majority of the problems that you face, is due to failing to manage expectations on the front end.

There are always problems with renovations and construction. You cannot eliminate those problems by only relying on what is put in the contract. The contract can only contain so much information, making it impossible to account for everything since every project is complex and unique by nature. The last thing you want to do is have to go to court to see who was right or wrong in the contract. Going to court is costly because of wasted resources, time, and opportunity costs. There are times to get lawyers involved but generally, when this happens, neither party comes out ahead.

Advice in Action #4: As the owner, project manager, or partner, it is your job to make sure that there are checks and balances in place to ensure that all parties involved are on the same page. Take the time to sit down and create a process that you can use to make sure your projects run smoothly every time. Here are some examples of the items in Chris's checks and balances system:

- **Ensures that all contractors are properly insured and licensed. He uses this process every time, whether he is hiring someone for a $100 job or a $100,000 job.**

- **Goes through the scope of work line by line with contractors up front**

- **Practices frequent communication**

- **When walking though the project with the contractor, he visualizes, details, and manages both his and the contractor's expectations**

- **While reviewing contractor bids, he knows that you typically get what you pay for in regards to quality and the ability to discuss and understand the projects expectations. It may be worth paying a little extra to have a contractor who is willing to work with you on managing these expectations vs. focusing on cost alone.**

Advice in Action #5: Another exercise that can help you identify areas where you need to create checks and balance systems for are as follows:

1. Create a list of mistakes, issues you've had with others, and any negative experiences you've had in your real estate career.

2. For the list above, ask yourself "what could I have done differently to have prevented _____ from happening?" Write down the answers.

   o If you don't know what you could have done differently, ask people who were in a similar situation but didn't have the checks and balances in place to learn how they handled it.

3. Now that you have potential solutions, create some sort of system that will ensure that you never make the same mistake again.

This section focuses on managing expectations with contractors, but you should take this advice and apply it to all aspects of your business.

In the next chapter, you will get two pieces of Best Ever Advice on:

1. The "big break" that launched a real estate career and how you can create a "big break" for yourself

2. Why you should "invest" in real estate instead of "trade" real estate

CHAPTER 4: INVEST INSTEAD OF TRADE

"Don't be afraid to give up the good to go for the great." – John D. Rockefeller

Best Ever Guest: Louis Rodriguez

Louis Rodriguez currently lives in New Orleans, LA, focusing on multifamily investments. He owns 16-unit, 37-unit, and 120-unit properties.

Episode 21

https://www.linkedin.com/in/rodriguezlouis

Louis has a fairly traditional real estate background, or what he likes to call "taking the scenic route." Looking back, he is sometimes surprised that he even decided to buy a single unit! After earning a bachelor's degree and a pair of master's degrees, Louis began working for a Fortune 500 company. With long hours spent in front of an Excel spreadsheet and dealing with the corporate policies, he quickly became quite miserable and had the realization that this kind of work was not congruent with what he wanted to do. As far back as 18 years old, Louis had a vision of real estate being a path to financial freedom. As a result, he was constantly reading and learning all he could about real estate growing up.

In 2005, Louis finally made the leap into real estate when he purchased a duplex outside of New Orleans, which he renovated, lived in one side, and rented out the other. Six months later, disaster hit. Hurricane Katrina hit New Orleans, which completely wiped out his first investment property. From a real estate standpoint, it was a total loss, but personally, many of Louis's family and friends lost a lot more. This put things in perspective. However, it was a rocky road, especially since it was his first investment. Looking back, Louis believes that without Katrina, he would not be where he is today as an investor. In the face of this crisis, Louis was inspired to rebuild the property. He persevered through the rebuilding process and overcame many of the fears that were holding him back from following his real estate plan.

After rebuilding his property, Louis left his corporate job, and set out to gain all the real estate knowledge he could. He worked in residential mortgage lending, took a job at a company doing capital placement for real estate developments, and worked as a commercial broker. Due to these experiences, Louis was able to weigh the pros and cons of the different real estate industries at a very high level, and ultimately selected multifamily as the asset type he would pursue. He got into the multifamily business on a small level, starting with a 16-unit property, and then scaling up to a 37-unit property followed by a 120-unit property.

Obviously, having his property wiped out by Hurricane Katrina was a huge learning experience. However, Louis believes that event which completely shifted his perspective about real estate led up to a "big break" he had while working in the commercial development industry.

The Big Break

Louis's "big break" occurred when he had the opportunity to apprentice under New Orleans most storied and prolific commercial developer. This was a difficult but incredible experience, where he learned the ins and outs of office space, retail space, single-family residences, hospitality, and multifamily. The experience and real estate knowledge that he gained was phenomenal. However, it was the perspective shift that had the most significant effect. By working with a self-made billionaire who started with nothing and seeing how he viewed the real estate world, Louis came out truly believing that he could do big things and the veil was finally lifted!

His big break was not something that he stumbled upon by luck. It was the result of proactively taking action. At the time, he was a mortgage broker and the industry was slowing down due to Katrina and the real estate crisis on the horizon. Louis wanted to get out of lending and gain some actual development and investment experience. He was ready to take it to the next level, so who better to show him the ropes than the best! Louis sought out the best real estate investor in New Orleans, who is someone he had never met, and wrote the investor an email outlining his goals, who he was, what he had been doing, and saying that he was really motivated to get more real estate experience. From this email, he was offered an interview. Louis was sent to an assessment center, where he was interviewed by 10 of the investor's team members, and was able to get the job. He was able to spend about 3 years with this investor, who was his new mentor, absorbing all the information and knowledge that he could.

Advice in Action #1: When Louis reached out to his mentor, he was not a total novice nor did he ask for guidance without offering anything in return. Instead, he provided a description of his background, his passion for real estate, and his interest in actually adding value to his mentor's real estate business. That being said, if you are on the hunt for a mentor, make sure you are offering something in return for the mentorship.

- **Outline your real estate goals**
- **Describe who you are and your real estate background**
- **Offer something of value that you can provide first, and then ask for guidance later!**

Invest Instead of Trade

Louis received many pieces of advice from his mentor and other real estate professionals. He was also exposed to a variety of different asset types and strategies. Some were extremely successful, while others did not work so well. The best advice he ever received did not come from his mentor, but from another successful investor with a massive multi-family portfolio valued at over a billion dollars. The advice was "never sell, never sell. You don't have to sell to succeed." Louis was perplexed by this advice due to its simplistic, old school nature, and its obsolescence. However, he knew he wanted to be as successful as this gentleman. He had reached the pinnacle of real estate success and had great credibility in the industry. Nevertheless, with such old school advice, Louis was curious as to why.

This gentleman gave Louis examples of people he knew, including Louis's mentor, who sold their assets over the course of 10, 20, or 30 years, and compared their levels of success with those who held on to their assets. After seeing the value of the long-term assets and the amount of cash flow they were generating, it opened his eyes. This gentleman also told Louis that he had never filed for bankruptcy, while Louis's mentor had faced bankruptcy multiple times. He was advising Louis to invest instead of trade and to focus on long-term growth instead of speculation.

What finally convinced Louis of the power of the "never sell" strategy was the following parable that this gentleman told him about a snowball and a mountain:

If you roll a snowball down a mountain, it starts off very small. As it begins to roll, it picks up more and more snow. Ultimately, the snowball that started off small will become bigger than the mountain itself.

This gentleman started off with a small snowball of just 2 units. Instead of discarding his snowball for a newer, bigger one, he just let the snowball continue to roll down the mountain and collect more snow. Rather than getting rid of properties he had purchased, he held on to them, and leveraged the equity to pick up more properties. The moral of the story is: unless the property is a terrible asset, use it to grow instead of buying and selling.

Advice in Action #2: Re-read the parable of the snowball and a mountain again and let its powerful message really sink in.

Louis asked more questions about how this gentleman "picked up more snow." He learned that he utilized his existing portfolio of assets, refinanced them tax free, and used the capital to purchase more properties. At this point, Louis had sold his initial portfolio containing 3 properties and used the profit to purchase a 16-unit property. After receiving this advice, instead of selling the 16-unit, Louis refinanced, pulled out the equity tax free, and used that cash to purchase a 37-unit property. He then repeated this same process to fund a large portion of the down payment for a 120-unit property, and has the intentions of using this strategy again to purchase a 250 to 500-unit apartment complex!

Action Item Advice in Action #3: Whether you are a new investor looking to purchase your first property, or an experienced investor that already has a sizable portfolio, when it comes time to sell, remember the parable of the snowball and the mountain. Instead of selling your property, consider refinancing tax-free and using the equity to scale up your business. You may not be able to pull out enough equity for a full down payment, but by keeping the property, you will be able benefit from the tax standpoint, continued cash flow, and long-term appreciation.

In the next chapter, you will get two pieces of Best Ever Advice on:

1. How to bounce back from losing $25,000 to then closing on over $20,000 worth of apartments

2. How to take a closer look at your personal expense in order to run a successful business

CHAPTER 5: BE PERSISTENT AND LEARN FROM FAILURES

"Do or do not. There is no try." – Yoda

Best Ever Guest: Jonathan Twombly

Jonathan Twombly is a managing member of Two Bridges Asset Management Company, which controls over 400 multifamily units. He runs The Mortar real estate blog, and is on the board of directors of the Harvard Real Estate Alumni Organization, Inc., a non-profit.

Episode 26

http://www.twobridgesmgmt.com

http://www.themortarblog.com

For the first part of his career, Jonathan worked as a lawyer who focused on litigation involving hotels and other commercial real estate assets. As time progressed, Jonathan became quite dissatisfied with being a lawyer due to a combination of long hours, stress, and it not being all that entrepreneurial. As a result, he began taking an interest in real estate investing. In his spare time, Jonathan would look up properties, analyze the financials, and fantasize about what life would be like as a real estate investor. He even went as far as going to some of the properties with his now partner.

Jonathan was a "victim" of the financial collapse, and in 2009, most of the law work he was doing began drying up. It took the law firm he was working for a couple of years to finally determine that the work wasn't coming back, so he was let go in 2011. Jonathan wasn't actually a "victim," because he was secretly hoping they would let him go due to his dissatisfaction with what he was doing as a lawyer. After being let go, Jonathan knew he did not want to find another law job. Instead, he really started focusing on real estate investing.

First Venture Into Real Estate Investing

Once Jonathan began focusing exclusively on real estate investing, he was able to network his way into a start-up multifamily investment partnership. He met a woman who owned a number of properties with her husband and was looking to scale her business from strictly family ownership to a real estate empire involving other investors. She told Jonathan "I know you don't have experience in this, but you seem like a smart guy with integrity. I think you can learn this so we should join up."

After forming this partnership, they began looking at potential assets in Louisiana and Texas, and found an owner who was selling 104-unit and 120-unit properties in Louisiana. They put the properties under contract, went through the due diligence process, and then right before closing, they learned that the bank they were using was dropping out. When they asked why, the bank told them it was due to the results of the inspection. However, the bank's reasons did not make sense. They said things like the inspector had found a golf ball that had come through a window in a vacant unit from the golf course next door. They said the breezeways were dirty, and they didn't like the fact that 10 units were not in rentable condition. But the down units were the "value add" upside to the property, and one of the reasons Jonathan and his partner saw value there. Jonathan believes the real reason the bank dropped out was due to the after-effects of the financial crisis. It was 2012 at the time, so banks weren't willing to take chances, and were looking for reasons not to fund deals.

Jonathan and his partner planned on using private money to fund the two deals. However, they had personally fronted all the due diligence costs. Since they lost the deals, both Jonathan and his partner were out about $25,000 each. It was a big financial blow, especially after working for a year with no income. At this point, they decided to go their separate ways.

Advice in Action #1: It is important to find the "good" that comes from experiencing failure. After losing these two deals, two "good" things that came out of it for Jonathan were:

1. **Not losing any investor money**

   - **This was a big factor. Since the investors didn't lose any of their money, they were still interested in investing with him moving forward.**

2. **Gaining a tremendous amount of learning**

   - **Even though he lost the deals, Jonathan still went through the due diligence process, lending, and all other aspects of a deal except the actual closing.**

After the dissolution of his first partnership, Jonathan sat down with an investor who was going to invest in the two apartment complexes and asked for advice on what to do next. During this conversation, the investor said that they should partner up, and Two Bridges Asset Management Company was formed. If it were not for the learning gained from the experience of losing the two deals and money, this investor wouldn't have had the confidence to partner with Jonathan for this venture. Even though the experience was painful at the time, it ended up being a tremendous opportunity in the end. It provided Jonathan with the foundational knowledge for what he is doing now, and it proved that he had persistence. Jonathan's track record showed that he wasn't going to run at the first sign of trouble. Two Bridges went on to buy more than

400 apartment units, worth approximately $20 million, in its first two years of business. They continue to attract new investors and new deals to their platform.

Advice in Action #2: You can never really fail. After losing these two deals and money, Jonathan realized that the reality of failing is not as bad as fearing failure. You need to put yourself into this mindset before you begin investing:

- **If you fail, you will live through it and come back to fight another day.**

- **If you keep on coming back, day after day after day, eventually, you will find success.**

Persistence

Jonathan's Best Ever advice is to be persistent. If you are going to be an entrepreneur, you can't ever give up. From starting his own business twice and failing once, Jonathan realized that the people who succeed don't do so because they have a brilliant idea, are super smart, or thought of something that no one else has thought of. They succeed because every time something goes wrong, they keep coming back and stick to it.

If you keep coming back to something long enough, eventually, you will catch a break. Therefore, it is vital that you put yourself in the position where you can stick to it. Many people go into business underfunded and have unrealistic expectations. As soon as their expectations aren't met or they face resistance, they give up. It is not because they have a bad idea or because they weren't smart. It is because they just gave up too soon. You never really know when success is going to meet you. It could be right around the corner, so if you don't stick to it and keep on going, you may never find out.

Advice in Action #3: Jonathan was in the position to be persistent in the face of failure because he:

- **Saved up a decent amount of money**
- **Doesn't own a car or most of the other things most people own**
- **Doesn't spend money on things he doesn't need**

Figure out what you need to do in order to put yourself in the position to stick to it, from a financial standpoint as well as by forming other important success habits.

The Important of Fiscal Prudence

Jonathan believes there is nothing better you can do for yourself, in regards to real estate and life in general, than live within your means and be fiscally prudent. When he was practicing law, he was shocked by the fact that his colleagues claimed to have no money. While he and his wife were living off of one salary, Jonathan had lawyer friends who were married to other lawyers, doctors, or highly paid individuals, but were always complaining about not having any money. When he talked to them about their lifestyles, Jonathan discovered they all had expensive cars, owned huge homes, and had many incredible expenses that he didn't think were necessary. Since Jonathan's needs were simple, he and his wife were able to live modestly and save money, and these character traits allowed him to be a successful entrepreneur.

Naturally wanting to save money is a great basis for being an entrepreneur. Nothing makes you happier than having a big bank account because it makes you feel secure. However, most people spend every dime that they make. If someone has an expensive, lavish personal life, then if they start a business, they will operate it the same way and end up spending themselves out of business.

Advice in Action #3: Do you live a fiscally prudent personal life or do you spend every dime you make? If you fall into the second category, it is extremely difficult to be a successful entrepreneur because you will end up over spending in your business too. Next time you want to buy something fancy or expensive, ask yourself if you really need it or if that money can be used more efficiently elsewhere.

In the next chapter, you will get four pieces of Best Ever Advice on:

1. A creative financing method for newbie investors

2. A step-by-step approach on raising money for your deals

3. Why you need to set your investment criteria and stick to it, no matter what

4. How to avoid the shiny object syndrome

CHAPTER 6: AVOID THE SHINY OBJECT SYNDROME

"I do not regret the things I've done, but those I did not do." –
Rory Cochrane

Best Ever Guest: Brie Schmidt

Brie Schmidt is the founder of BBS Apartments, which invests in multifamily properties in Chicago and Milwaukee. She has also been a real estate broker for 10 years.

Episode 48

http://www.turnkey-reviews.com

Brie got started in real estate when she obtained her real estate license in 2004. After a little less than a year, she realized that she hated being a real estate agent. Brie didn't like dealing with first-time homebuyers or the emotional buyers. Therefore, in 2005, she left real estate and took a corporate sales job. She always kept her license as a back-up plan so if anything were to happen with her corporate sales job, she knew she could always go back into real estate.

In 2010, Brie and her husband began searching for their first property in Chicago. They quickly discovered that it was actually cheaper to purchase a 2800 square-foot three unit multifamily than it was to purchase a 1500 square-foot single-family residence. They decided it made sense financially to go the multifamily route with the intentions to eventually convert it into the home of their dreams.

When they initially purchased the property, Brie never thought she would end up becoming a real estate investor. However, being a landlord ended up being a lot easier than she had expected. As a result, during the next four years, Brie and her husband acquired additional units, bringing their total to 59 units. In 2015, she started working with partners and acquired an additional 21 units, bringing her total to 80 units.

Creative Financing

Since Brie and her husband planned on living in the three-unit property, they were able to obtain a 3.5% down FHA loan. The property was recently rehabbed with granite countertops, stainless steel appliances, and other amenities, so the initial and ongoing expenses were very low. After putting two tenants in place, they were able to live for free because the rent they collected every month covered their monthly expenses.

Advice in Action #1: If you are looking for a way to get into the real estate game, but do not have a significant amount of money saved up, consider following Brie's entry strategy. Find a two to four unit multifamily property and commit to living in one unit and renting out the others. This enables you to qualify for a 3.5% down FHA loan. You will be able to get your first property for very little money down and you will be able to live for free or at a discount since the tenants are covering the mortgage. If the property requires major repairs, no problem. Another loan program, the 203k FHA loan, allows you to include the renovation costs in the loan. You will put down 3.5% of the purchase price plus renovations instead of having to pay for the renovations out of pocket.

With the one and a half year break between purchasing the first and second properties, Brie and her husband were able to save up a significant amount of money, which they used to purchase the additional 24 units with conventional residential and commercial loans. At the moment, Brie says "if we were looking to buy at the same pace, I think my husband would kill me!" She had to promise her husband that there would be a stopping point because he was afraid that she would never stop. Unfortunately, they were in the situation where they were financially tapped out and couldn't continue to fund deals personally. Brie and her husband were planning to acquire another 8 to 10 properties in 2015, so they had to brainstorm creative methods to finance these purchases.

After speaking with family and friends, she discovered that her brother had a significant amount of equity in his personal home. Due to Brie's prior successful deals, her brother was confident enough to agree to pull the equity out of his house and give her the money to invest for one year. Brie will use this money as a down payment assuming that she can pay her brother back in a year. The loan is only going to cover a portion of the down payment. The remaining balance of the down payment will be covered with money Brie and her husband accumulated from their jobs and the income from the other properties in her portfolio.

Brie's current market is Milwaukee, Wisconsin. The last deal that she purchased was a package of properties. Brie purchased them for slightly over $500,000 with a gross rental income of a little over $12,000 per month. This results in around a 14% cap rate. If she can replicate this deal, the resulting cash flow, in combination with the cash flow from her other properties, would be enough to pay back the loan.

Advice in Action #2: You will eventually get to a point in your real estate career where you are either tapped out of funds or have obtained the maximum amount of conventional loans. This is an obstacle that a majority of investors will face, but it doesn't mean your real estate career is over. In the same way that Brie was creative and was able to obtain a loan from her brother, you will also need to use your creativity to overcome this hurdle.

- **Create a list of everyone you know**

- **Sort them into different categories (family, friends, works, etc.)**

- **Next to each of their names, write down how much money you believe they would be willing to invest.**

- **The goal is to get one person from each category interested in investing**

- **Once you get one person interested, you can name-drop that person to the other people in that category.**

It is important to keep in mind that if you personally only have enough funds to cover a portion of the down payment, you can still use the method above to cover the rest.

Instead of creating a document, you can email info@joefairless.com and put "Investor Spreadsheet" as the subject. You will receive the spreadsheet that I use to raise millions of dollars for my apartment communities.

Know Your Floor and Stick With It

Brie's best advice ever is to "know your floor, and stick with it." A floor is an investment rule that you set which you commit to never going breaking. Your floor can be quantitative (i.e. cash on cash return, cap rate, price point, rehabs over $XX, XXX, etc.) or qualitative (foundation issues, neighborhood class, property type, etc.). She is personally facing this situation, since she is looking for a property to use her brother's loan on, and as a broker, she goes through this with her clients all the time.

Since Brie took the loan from her brother with the understanding that the loan had to be repaid in a year, she has to be picky, know her market, and stick to her 14% cap rate floor when seeking out potential deals. However, she is very excited to buy something so she can be done with it and take a break for a while. As a result, she is finding herself looking at properties that are below her floor. In reality, Brie knows that she needs to walk away from it and stick to her floor. Even if it is a smaller buy than expected, she still needs to stick to those numbers, even if it is an emotionally difficult thing to do.

Brie also has to reinforce this advice with her clients all the time. This includes working with first-time homebuyers or people looking to purchase a multifamily and live in one unit while renting out the others. Sometimes they are so excited to officially become a homeowner or a real estate investor, they stretch the numbers, tweak the deal, and lie to themselves in order to make the numbers work to justify the buy. Joe was guilty of doing this on his first multifamily deal. It is a lesson that he only needed to learn once.

When setting a floor, everyone has different objectives. It can be a wide variety of things since each market and situation is unique. Therefore, it really depends on the person. For Brie, she has set her floor at a 14% cap rate in Milwaukee and a 10% cap rate in Chicago. For her clients, their floor may be a property that fits within a specific budget, or a multifamily that allows them to have the tenants cover the mortgage so they can live rent-free. The point is: you have to decide what your floor is, stick to it no matter what, and know how to walk away and be patient for the next one.

Advice in Action #3: Do you know what your floor is? If so, great, commit to sticking to it. If not, sit down and figure out what your floor is:

- **Write down what your real estate objective is.**

- **Figure out what criteria a property needs to meet in order for you to meet this objective.**

- **Write down the following statement, inserting your objective and your floor into the blanks: "I know that my real estate objective is _____. In order to reach this objective, I must buy a property that is above my floor, which is**

_____. **I commit to sticking to this floor. If a property is below _____, then I need to walk away."**

Sometimes, looking for real estate can be frustrating. It took Brie and her husband 7 months to find their first property and it was an exhausting experience. They were worn down and wanted a deal so badly that they probably would have taken almost anything, so they had to take a step back. They had to remind themselves that they couldn't compromise their goals. If the numbers are bad and the property is bad, then the deal is bad, and you have to walk away.

Avoid Shiny Object Syndrome

There are many different opportunities in real estate. The longer you are in the industry, the more people you get to know, and the better your track record gets, the greater variety of opportunities you get presented with. It is incredibly important for you to stick to your floor, know exactly what approach you are going to take, and not to get distracted by shiny objects.

Here's a situation that Brie faced when she got an inspection report back on a property in Milwaukee. The inspector discovered that the whole basement had structural foundation issues, which would require a significant amount of money to repair. After adding this expense and re-running the numbers, Brie saw that if the costs came back as expected, it would still be a profitable deal. However, since the cost was just an initial estimate, the numbers could more than double if the issue turned out to be more severe. More importantly, Brie doesn't buy properties that involve structural issues or mold problems, so she was able to avoid falling into the "shiny object syndrome" trap and walked away.

Advice in Action #4: To put this situation into perspective, Brie was quoted $20,000 as the price to rebuild the basement. If you were to purchase a $100,000 property at 20% down, you would also need to spend $20,000.

- Would you rather invest $20,000 to fix a foundation problem or would you rather use that money to invest in a $100,000 property?

If you find yourself falling into the "shiny object syndrome" trap and are contemplating spending a large portion of money on something, ask yourself:

- Is there a better investment I could make with this same amount of money that would result in higher returns?

Maybe you could use it as a down payment, or to update the kitchens of another one of your rental units, etc.

In the next chapter, you will get three pieces of Best Ever Advice on:

1. How to build a full-scale real estate investment business and leave your full-time job

2. How you can start doing bigger deals with the same number of resources you currently have at your disposal

3. How to do bigger deals

CHAPTER 7: SCALING QUICKLY

"Treat your customers like they own you, because they do!" –
Mark Cuban

Best Ever Guest: Chris Urso

Chris Urso is the co-founder of URS Capital Partners and Elite
Apartment Coaching, a multifamily education and consulting firm,
dedicated to creating lasting wealth by investing in apartments. In the
last 4 years, his company has acquired over $70 million worth of apart-
ments. Chris has also personally raised over $22 million of private
capital, working with over 200 investors.

Episode 51

http://www.eliteapartmentcoaching.com

Chris got started in real estate in 2001. At that point, Chris did not really
have any real estate experience, other than reading a couple of books
right after college. A natural entrepreneur at heart, real estate struck
a chord with him, creating not just passive income for himself, but a
business that he could grow over time. Chris was working for a non-real
estate related company in Manhattan doing document management
and litigation support for Manhattan law firms and used his salary to
purchase his first rental property, a duplex, at the age of 22. For the next
7 years, he continued to work in the city, while growing his real estate
portfolio. During this time, Chris helped grow the litigation support

company from 10 to 300 employees, and continued to grow his real estate business by acquiring residential rental properties, doing fix and flips, and participating in a few new construction projects.

In 2007, Chris saw that the entire market was shifting and simultaneously, the company he worked for was being sold. Chris decided it was time to sell all of his personal real estate holdings. He had done really well for the past 7 years and had the foresight to get out of the market before the financial crisis hit. At this point, Chris and his wife faced a fork in the road.

Were they going to spend the rest of their lives in Corporate America or were they going to pursue real estate full-time?

The fact that his wife had made the move to pursue real estate full-time three years earlier made this decision easier. She had left a successful career at the New York Federal Reserve Bank, went to NYU and obtained a Master Degree in Real Estate (paid for by her real estate transactions), becoming a full-time real estate broker, focusing specifically on investor transactions.

In 2008 during the heart of the downturn, Chris decided to join his wife and take the dive into real estate full-time. He, therefore, founded URS Capital Partners. As a team, they were able to navigate this difficult time period with a clear vision of where their company needed to go. They have faced challenges along the way but are very grateful and fortunate to be where they are today.

With experience in both the residential and multifamily side, Chris knew that to scale his business successfully, his path to success was in apartments. From this point forward, he only focused on residential multifamily, not retail, office, strip centers, SFRs, etc. By honing in on larger apartment deals and focusing on adding value, Chris was able to scale his business quickly and organically over the following 4 years, controlling over 1,300 multifamily units throughout the Southeast and Midwest. Chris's largest acquisition to date is a $14.04M complex. His passion is helping middle to high-income individuals establish a personal plan to build wealth, preserve their capital and ultimately create a family legacy through investing in multifamily real estate.

Add Value, Sell Quickly

Over the years, Chris has done over 60 real estate deals ranging from inexpensive $20,000 houses to $500,000 brownstones in Brooklyn, to $14 million apartment deals. The best advice he received on how to build a full-scale real estate investment business and leave a full-time job, *or* how to expand a current business, is to focus on value-add deals. Value-add deals are situations where you buy at a discount, create value, and sell them for a profit as fast as possible (this is the key to real growth). When Chris received this advice, it changed the way he looked at everything in his investment business, from his entire thought process to the types of deals he focused on. Chris attributes this mindset change to what has really fueled his company's rapid growth.

Advice in Action #1: This advice can be applied no matter where you are in your real estate journey, but really holds true when you are raising money from investors for two main reasons:

1. **It is great to make a return year-over-year and month-over-month, but demonstrating to investors that you can execute a transaction from start to finish *and* make a sizable profit in a relatively short window of time, is going to allow you to really grow. Your investors will follow you to the next deal, and they will start talking to their friends and families more confidently, which in turn, will lead to more investors.**

2. **Bigger investors will view you as a serious real estate professional because you can go from A to Z, execute your business plan, and make a profit.**

Adding value and selling quickly is a tough concept to understand and comprehend when first starting out. There are a few examples of common traps that Chris has seen clients and even himself fall into:

- *"If I buy something, I don't want to let it go," because you here the "buy-and-hold" strategy all the time.*

- *When Chris was initially investing in single-family residences, he purchased properties that were move-in ready, so he didn't have to put a lot of money into renovations.*

- *He has many private clients come to him with the idea of buying a property and holding it for 20 years - this is always dependent on the personal goals of the client.*

Chris discovered that if you want to transition from single-family or small multifamily investing to apartment investing, you have to shift your mentality from a "turnkey, long-term hold" to a "value-add, sell quickly" mindset. If you buy a turnkey property because it is already performing as well as it can, there likely is not likely to be much value that can be created. If you want to raise capital for deals, your investors will expect a large profit that comes as a result of a sale.

Advice in Action #2: You do not have to apply this mentality to all of your goals. Everyone has personal goals (long-term profit for you and your family) and business goals (quick profit for investors and yourself). You can work both plans at the same time, but keep in mind that these goals are accomplished by following completely different business plans. Make sure that you have different business plans with the types of deals you are going to be acquiring to achieve your personal and business goals.

After four years of scaling his business by adding value, selling quickly, and repeating, usually with pretty gritty deals, Chris was able to close on the prettiest property he has ever acquired, a $12.4 million 228-unit B Class apartment complex. The units featured granite countertops, a new pool, fitness center, clubhouse, tennis court, and basketball court.

With all of these amazing amenities, Chris was still able to stay true to the added-value component, because the property had operational challenges. The previous owners were a group of single-family investors and this was their first larger apartment complex. When they purchased the property, they put millions of dollars into renovations like they would a single-family home, and over-improved the interiors. While they did a nice job of repositioning the property from a physical perspective, operationally the financials were not operating near their full potential. The deal was running at occupancy levels 5% less than market and offering unnecessarily aggressive concessions. Chris immediately saw that they were leaving a lot of money on the table. Thanks to the interior improvements of the previous owners paired with Chris' strategic amenity upgrades, they were able to not spend much towards renovations, yet dramatically change the performance of the asset.

Advice in Action #3: A $12.4 million property may seem like it is something outside the realm of possibility for you, but Chris thought the same thing when he just started out with a duplex. If you can purchase value-add opportunities, sell relatively quickly, and repeat the process, you will be doing $12.4 million deals and beyond in no time.

Focus on Bigger Deals

If your goals do not involve creating a huge real estate business, Chris believes it is still important to focus on bigger, higher rewarding deals. Chris learned this the hard way by initially investing in really inexpensive houses and having to work very hard for a little return. This piece of advice is also a challenge to grasp for people coming right out of the gate. This is because a "bigger deal" is relative to an individual's perception of what a big deal is. A big deal may be 6-units to one person and 100-units to someone else - everyone's resources and goals are completely different.

Advice in Action #4: Look at where you are at in your real estate journey and see what resources you have at your disposal. Potential resources include:

- **Cash**
- **Your time**
- **Your skillset**
- **People you might know**
- **Your resourcefulness**

Many people create business plans that focus solely on cash, so make that sure you are leveraging all of the resources you have at your disposal.

One example is when a client came to Chris with a goal of purchasing a single-family plus a 2-unit property in Year One, and then purchasing a 4-unit plus a 6-unit in Year Two, for a total of 13 units. The first question he asked was "do you think it makes a little bit more sense to spend one year getting educated in real estate, truly understanding and absorbing it, and then do a 20-unit deal in Year Two with the same resources at your disposal?"

Advice in Action #5: Start smart, invest in yourself, and get the knowledge you need to identify the best deals. No matter where you are at, if you plan on doing one deal a year, make sure that it counts and is aligned with your goal.

Another example is when a client came to Chris with $1 million and was looking to purchase a property using all cash. He told his client to take a deep breath, and explained the unbelievable financing options available in today's market. Instead of purchasing a $1 million property for cash, he asked "what if we took that $1 million and used it as a down payment for a very conservative $3 million property so you are not overleveraged?" Both scenarios required the same resources on the front end, $1 million, but both have a completely different end result. In the first scenario, the client would purchase a $1 million, 30 to 40-unit apartment complex. In the second scenario, the client would purchase a $3 million, 140-unit building. You would think that the second scenario would be the risker of the two. However, having more units under one roof (economies of scale) can result in a more efficiently run property and mitigates your risk.

Advice in Action #6: In this example, Chris's client was able to leverage his cash to scale up, but you can do the same thing with the other resources you have at your disposal. For the list of resources you created earlier, brainstorm ways you can leverage these resources to scale your business. For example, if your goal is to purchase a 10-unit property this year, join forces with someone you know who has a similar goal, and purchase a 30-unit property together instead. This mindset of "thinking bigger" may be a slightly slower process, but the future rewards are FAR greater.

In the next chapter, you will get the Best Ever Advice on:

1. A five step-by-step blueprint for how to achieve the investor's Holy Grail, financial independence

CHAPTER 8: THE 5-STEP BLUEPRINT TO FINANCIAL INDEPENDENCE IN 3 YEARS

"Screw it. Let's do it." – Richard Branson

Best Ever Guest: Joseph Le

Joseph Le rehabbed and rented out his 8th property in 2014, which allowed him to replace his income from his full-time job.

Episode 90

http://www.newrenthome.com

Joseph started in real estate in 2011, when he got married and began discussing with his new wife what they would do with their money to secure a financially independent future. They decided the best thing to do was real estate because many people that they knew were successful in real estate. Joseph and his wife took the money they received from their wedding and purchased their first property. It was pretty scary at first but every day, they took persistent and consistent action to get them to where they wanted to be. Eight investments later, they were having a great time and couldn't be happier. The 8th property allowed them to reach the investor's holy grail of replacing their incomes with passive real estate income. This was a HUGE accomplishment for them.

When Joseph and his wife set out for the investor's Holy Grail, they both had full-time jobs. The original reason for wanting to replace their incomes with real estate was to start a family and have his wife stay at home to take care of the children. Once they finally reached their goal, they just had their first child, but Joseph's wife really liked her job, so she decided to stay while they continued to invest.

The 5-Step Blueprint to Financial Independence

When Joseph and his wife first got started, they used some of their savings to purchase properties, but the key to their quick success was leverage. The following is the five-step process they used as a blueprint to their financial independence and as an example, we will look at a typical deal that Joseph and his wife would purchase.

<u>The Example Deal</u>

- *Purchase Price - $50,000*

- *Required Renovations - $20,000*

- *After-repair value (ARV) - $100,000*

<u>The 5-Step Blueprint to Financial Independence</u>

1. *Hard Money Lender*

    o Joseph and his wife used hard money loans to finance the properties. They would go to a hard moneylender and tell them how much the property cost, the estimated rehab costs, and the estimated ARV.

    o Typically, the hard moneylender would provide a loan for 70% of the ARV.

2. *Rehab*

    o Rehab the property

    o Joseph and his wife aimed for a project time of 2 to 3 weeks max

3. *Rented Out*

    o Get the property rented out

4. *Refinance*

   o   Refinance the property with a conventional loan

   o   Pay back the hard moneylender

5. *Repeat*

   o   Start the process all over again

Advice in Action #1: By repeating this same process 8 times, Joseph was able to achieve the investor's Holy Grail in three short years. If your goal is to replace your full-time income, use the following process to outline what you need to do in order to achieve this:

- **Determine what your monthly income is from your full-time job before taxes.** 3,000

- **Determine how many rental properties you need to acquire based on your personal investment criteria.** 3

- **Create a timeline for how often you will purchase properties.** 1 yr

Advice in Action #2: Keep track of your debt-to-income ratio. This should not be a problem when you are obtaining a hard money loan, but you may run into problems when you are refinancing into a traditional loan. Another thing to look out for is the maximum number of loans that the traditional bank you chose allows. If the bank will only provide four loans, make sure that your plan reflects this. Try to find a lender, like a portfolio lender, that does not have a cap on the number of loans you can get or reach out to a commercial lender to see if they will combine multiple mortgage loans into one large loan.

If the numbers work out right, having a deal with no money out of pocket is totally doable. For the example above, since the hard moneylender loans 70% of the ARV, Joseph and his wife would get a loan for $70,000 ($100,000 ARV x 70% = $70,000), which covers the purchase price and rehab costs. With the ARV at $100,000, they would refinance to a 70% LTV (loan-to-value) conventional loan, pay back the hard moneylender, and have a rental property with no money out of their pockets! Joseph says that the key is finding a property you can acquire that has a good spread so after you perform the improvements, you'll have a large chunk of equity.

Advice in Action #3: You need to have a full-time job if you want to easily obtain a traditional loan to cash out the hard moneylender. Even if you do not plan on following Joseph hard money strategy, having a job is a great back up or supplement so you do not have to rely on hustling or cutting corners. While there is nothing inherently wrong with hustling, the path to financial freedom can be a lot easier if you still have a full-time job. It is necessary when it comes to both obtaining financing and having an extra income stream to purchase additional properties faster.

Another piece of this blueprint Joseph believes is important is to hire out a general contractor to do rehabs. When Joseph and his wife first started, they thought they could do some or most of the work themselves. They thought they were saving money, but quickly realized that by performing the renovations themselves, they were actually losing money. The key is not just saving money, but also saving time. Joseph and his wife were not professionals rehabbers, so they would rather have someone who knew what they were doing, could do the rehabs quickly, and do it right the first time so they could get the property rented as quickly as possible.

Advice in Action #4: Hire out general contractors to perform the renovations. Otherwise, you are spending a lot of time and effort, and creating frustrations that do not make the business fun (unless you're into that sort of thing). Hiring out the work not only makes the process more fun, but also puts more money in your pocket.

Wrapping up Part One

In Part One, you received the Best Ever Buy-and-Hold Advice from eight successful real estate professionals.

In Part Two, you will receive the Best Ever Fix-and-Flip advice from three successful fix-and-flippers, as well as action items you can immediately implement to improve your fix-and-flip business. To begin, you will get four pieces of Best Ever Advice on:

1. The benefits of buying and selling vacant land, as well as common misconceptions

2. How to find motivated sellers using a county's delinquent tax list

3. Why challenging your assumptions when analyzing a properties financials will keep you out of trouble

PART TWO:

THE BEST FIX-AND-FLIP INVESTING ADVICE EVER

CHAPTER 9: MAKING MONEY BY FLIPPING LAND

"Our greatest fear should not be of failure but of succeeding at things in life that don't really matter." – Francis Chan

Best Ever Guest: Seth Williams

Seth Williams is the founder of REtipster, a real estate investing blog for part-time investors. All of his investing has been done part-time. Seth also has nearly 10 years of experience as a commercial real estate banker, closing on hundreds of transactions.

Episode 60

http://www.REtipster.com/

In 2008, Seth began investing in real estate part-time while continuing to work a full-time job. When starting out, he was searching for properties strictly on the MLS, which created a consistent problem. Seth would analyze the financials using the MLS listing price, but was having difficulties finding a good deal. Even if he decreased the list price, the deal still didn't make financial sense. He quickly learned that if he wanted to find a good deal, he would have to search outside the MLS.

Seth set out to find a real estate investment strategy where he could find owners who would be highly motivated. He needed a strategy where they didn't care about their properties, could no longer afford them, or just didn't want them. One such strategy that fit the bill was targeting property owners who were on the delinquent tax list. Seth went to the county treasurer's office, obtained the delinquent tax list, which contained the information of everyone in the county who was currently delinquent on property taxes, and sent out a mailing campaign.

Surprisingly, a good number of the entries on the list were not typical real estate properties, but vacant land. Seth figured that since the owners were delinquent on their taxes, he could purchase the vacant land for a cheap price, turn them around, and make a decent profit. Seth had finally found his niche in the real estate market, and he has been buying and selling vacant land as his main source of business ever since.

Benefits of Flipping Vacant Land

Vacant land has almost none of the hassles associated with typical real estate properties. There is no one living there, there is nothing to break down, and there is nothing to steal. Vacant land is the pinnacle of low maintenance real estate. A landowner can let their properties sit unattended for years on end without worrying about the condition of their property. The combination of these benefits is why buying and selling vacant land was so appealing to Seth. On top of that, since the owners of the land were delinquent on their taxes, Seth could purchase them for really good prices.

The first deal Seth got from his mailer was a half-acre lot about an hour outside of his metro area. He offered only $331 and the owner accepted. Seth closed on the property and sold it two weeks later for $1900. Even though these were not huge numbers, when Seth completed the deal, he thought it was crazy! In a matter of weeks, he was able to make almost a couple thousand dollars with minimal risk and no need for a loan.

After this first deal, Seth figured that he didn't have to stay with cheap land because there had to be plenty of vacant land out there that was a worth a lot more than $300. He followed the same offer structure from his first deal, offering a small percentage of what the land would actually sell for. As a result, Seth found many opportunities for getting vacant land for next to nothing and didn't require obtaining a loan from a bank.

Advice in Action #1: Not every owner of vacant land, or real estate in general, who is motivated will accept the low offers. It is a numbers game. If you submit enough offers, you will find that a lot of people will accept them in time, even if they reject the offer initially. You may submit an offer today and get rejected, but if you keep at it, they may come back a few months later asking if your offer still stands. Don't give up at the first sign of resistance or you may end up missing out on some great opportunities

Obtaining Delinquent Tax Lists

When Seth first started out, he didn't have to physically go to the county treasurer's office to obtain the delinquent tax list. All he had to do was pick up the phone, call in, and politely ask for the list. However, the process isn't as simple for every situation. Sometimes, Seth would call the county treasurer and they either wouldn't give him the list or didn't understand what he was asking for. In these situations, he has to use other means to obtain the tax list, and unfortunately, it usually isn't free. Some counties will sell their delinquent tax lists for $0.01 per parcel, while others will charge upwards of $1.50 per parcel. Seth has never paid more than $400 to $500, so if a list costs more, he will pass.

Advice in Action #2: Since you can obtain delinquent tax lists without requesting them in person, it allows you to potentially invest in vacant land out-of-state. Go online, look up the county treasurer's contact information, and give them a call. If they won't give you the list, either find another county, or figure out how you can buy the list by conducting research on the Internet.

Are There Disadvantages to Flipping Land?

Misconception #1: No Cash Flow

One of the biggest misconceptions is when there isn't a structure on the land, there won't be any cash flow. In reality, Seth has not found this to be the case. He has purchased several properties for a fraction of their market value (anywhere from 10% to 30% of what they would sell for on the open market), and resold them at a significant mark up from his purchase price with seller financing. Since these buyers are purchasing at a price closer to the property's fair market value, most of them will gladly pay more for their initial down payment than Seth paid for his entire acquisition of the property, which means the subsequent years of monthly payments are pure profit. Essentially, these seller financed vacant land properties produce income just like rental properties do, but with none of the headaches most rental properties are known for.

Misconception #2: Environmental and Zoning Issues

To combat potential environmental or zoning issues, Seth always performs the required due diligence before closing. He also focuses on residential vacant land, which isn't subject to most of the environmental laws that affects commercial properties.

Misconception #3: Can't Write Off Depreciation

Since there is not a structure on the land, there is nothing to write off as depreciation. For Seth, this is not a big deal because of the advantages of not having to get a loan and having very minimal expenses compared to a typical real estate property transaction.

Aside from these three misconceptions, Seth has run into two other difficulties in regards to buying and selling vacant land. First, establishing the market value of vacant land is surprisingly difficult, which makes the rest of the process harder. Unlike a typical real estate listing, there are not a lot of comps for vacant land and most vacant land properties don't produce rental income, so the standard valuation processes do not apply. Seth has discovered it is an art and a science when it comes to calculating the value of the land.

A second issue Seth has faced is that sometimes he can sell within a few weeks, while other times, it takes much longer. The longest time it has taken him to sell a piece of land was approximately one year, but most of the time, the sales process is completed within a few months. When working with vacant land, the fact that there is little competition is great as a buyer, but not so much as a seller. In general, there are fewer land buyers out there. There is always a specific buyer out there who will gladly pay your asking price, but sometimes it takes a while to find them because they aren't sitting on every corner. You have to go out and find where these buyers are and give them the information they need to make a purchasing decision.

Advice in Action #2: No matter which real estate niche you decide to invest in, there will always be disadvantages. This also holds true for flipping land. However, most are simply perceived as disadvantages. For Seth, he was able to use these misconceptions to his advantage by thinking creatively:

- **He has never come across any competition, unlike a typical real estate transaction where dozens of investors are involved.**
- **He has never had to fight with another investor when submitting his offers**
- **Since it is just him and the seller, they do not really have any other options**

When you face a disadvantage or difficulties in your real estate investing career, instead of turning away, take the time to figure out if it is a true problem or if there is a way you can spin it to you advantage.

Always Challenge Your Assumptions

Seth's Best Ever advice is whenever you are evaluating a deal, whether you are buying a rental property, a flip, or a piece of land, always challenge your assumptions and make them as conservative as possible. When he decided to give rental property investing a try, he was working with a realtor who was giving him pie in the sky numbers. In this case, the numbers were so unrealistic that Seth was able to catch it early. If he had taken everything this realtor was saying as truth, he would have been in deep trouble.

It is important to remember that a realtor's main motivation is to sell the property, not necessarily to provide the best possible investment. If you fall for this trap, don't blame the realtor. The higher they sell the property, the more they get paid, so it's hard to fault a person for doing what's in their best interests.

Advice in Action #3: When you think you have the correct inputs and assumptions for your financial analysis, ask yourself "what makes me think these numbers are correct?" Really dig into the numbers and understand where they are coming from. Your inputs determine everything on the back end, so if you have the wrong information, you are going to have major issues.

In the next chapter, you will get three pieces of Best Ever Advice on:

1. How to creatively invest in real estate, no matter how bad your current financial situation is

2. Lessons learned from being conned by a con man

3. Common examples of when using eraser math can get you into trouble

CHAPTER 10: GETTING CONNED BY A CON MAN

"He who aims at the sun, though he is sure to miss it, hits higher than he who aims at the ground." – Glenn's Mother

Best Ever Guest: Glenn and Amber Schworm

Glenn and Amber Schworm are the founders of Signature Home Buyers, a real estate fix and flip business in Upstate New York.

Episode 62

http://www.signaturehomebuyers.com

Glenn and Amber got started in real estate in 2007, when the real estate market was in the beginning stages of crisis. While everyone else was running for the hills and getting out of real estate, Glenn and Amber were in a position where they had to make a move. They went to a local real estate seminar with a speaker whom had done 250 flips, which seemed like an unreachable number because they hadn't even done one deal yet.

Glenn and Amber immediately started applying the principles they learned from the seminar and purchased their first flip. It took about seven months to complete, but they ended up making a $17,000 profit. Their second fix-and-flip was in 2008, which was the middle of the downturn. Glenn and Amber performed the renovations themselves, working 15-18 hour days for 33 straight days. All of this hard work paid off when they were able to sell the property in a bidding war for $2,000 over asking price, clearing a $35,000 profit, all while the market was tanking. At this point, they were hooked. Glenn and Amber realized that maybe they were on to something, so they stopped everything else they were doing and focused exclusively on real estate. Since then, Glenn and Amber have flipped 300 homes and founded Signature Home Buyers, where they have 4 agents and 5 other employees working for them.

Glenn and Amber have come a long way in a short amount of time, but to them, it does not always feel that way. They have learned a lot from overcoming many obstacles and making even more mistakes. Glenn and Amber believe that we should all learn from other people's mistakes, but some of the best learning experiences come from making our own. When facing an obstacle or making a mistake, it is important to learn from it so it doesn't happen again and then move forward as quickly as possible.

$80,000 in Credit Card Debt

When they purchased their first property, Glenn and Amber had $80,000 in credit card debt. At the time, they were able to get a No Doc loan (doesn't require the borrower to provide income to lender) to cover the purchase price and used credit cards to fund the renovations. Due to already being $80,000 in credit card debt, Glenn and Amber did not have enough credit available to afford all of the renovations, even though they were doing most of the work themselves. Luckily, Amber had a Mercedes worth $10,000, so they sold the vehicle and used the cash to complete the flip. All said and done, they were able to make $17,000 in profit.

To fund more deals, Glenn and Amber began searching for private investors. Their first investor was a friend whom had a large amount of equity in their home. From here, they have raised over $3 million from private investors, including this friend, who is still an investor to this day.

Advice in Action #1: Glenn and Amber used their creativity to figure out "how" they could get into real estate. Not only did they not have any money, but they were also $80,000 in the hole! Glenn and Amber leveraged the equity in a personal vehicle, used left over lines of credit, and raised money from a friend to purchase their first two deals. Moving forward, ask yourself "how" you can do something instead of making excuses as to why you "can't" do something. This will get your creative juices flowing and help you solve any that problem you come across.

Conned by a Professional Con Man

A few years ago, Glenn and Amber purchased 10 properties with a plan to renovate all of them in 30 days. At the same time, a 70 year-old man, (let's call him Bob) had been calling them for about a year asking to give them a hand with project management. With taking on 10 properties at once, and with Amber being pregnant, they saw this as a perfect opportunity to give Bob a chance to help in such a busy time. Over the course of the next 9 weeks, Glenn and Amber paid Bob over $200,000 to manage all 10 projects. About 3 to 4 weeks into the project, Glenn and Amber suspected something was awry with Bob, but due to other problems, a baby on the way, and 10 projects going on simultaneously, he let it go another 5 weeks.

At the 9-week point, Glenn and Amber went to visit one of the properties that Bob was managing and found that the property was torn almost all the way to the ground. They also discovered that Bob had pocketed over half of the $200,000 they had given him, so they realized they were being teed up for a major con. Glenn and Amber always do background checks on everyone who comes into their company, but due to the casual nature of the relationship, in this case they did not. At this point, Glenn and Amber conducted a background check and found out Bob had done 5 years in federal prison for grand larceny, with one year in solitary confinement. This was a sobering moment because Bob was in their home and around their family. This realization did some major damage. As a result, Glenn and Amber instantly fired Bob and then an all-out war broke out.

Bob was trying to shake them down for hundreds of thousands of dollars by putting fake liens on their properties. Bob also broke into Glenn and Amber's office, got all of their investor's phone numbers, and began calling them saying Glenn and Amber were running a Ponzi scheme. Luckily, they had built a solid reputation and had always demonstrated integrity and character. Therefore, all of their investors stood behind them. In retrospect, Glenn and Amber remember a moment when they were at home and came to the realization that they were dealing with a professional con man. They put their heads together and Glenn said, "We have two choices. We can either quit or we can fight and grow and make this problem go away." Knowing Glenn so well, Amber already knew they were going to fight. That night, they decided to learn from this mistake and grow, which really pushed them to overcome this obstacle. Glenn and Amber hired lawyers, fought Bob's false accusations, and ultimately won the war. They ended up losing hundreds of thousands of dollars through this whole ordeal, but they learned some very valuable lessons, and more importantly, they survived.

The most ironic and satisfying aspect of this story is when Bob threatened Glenn and Amber that if they didn't pay him the hundreds of thousands of dollars, he was going to call the local business newspaper and tell them Glenn and Amber were frauds. They told Bob they would let their record speak for itself. One year later, Glenn and Amber received a call from the very same paper, and ended up being in an article on the front page of the paper as one of the top flippers in the area.

Advice in Action #2: In this situation, Glenn and Amber's biggest mistake was not doing a simple $25 background check on the front end. No matter what, commit to always doing background checks.

Another lesson of this story is to trust your gut. Glenn and Amber had a feeling something was awry with Bob after 3-4 weeks, but unfortunately did not act on this feeling for another month. Commit to following your gut, because simple mistakes can end up being deadly.

Don't Use Eraser Math

When calculating what you are going to do in any real estate business model, Glenn and Amber's best advice is to be honest, don't lie, and never use eraser math. Over the years doing hundreds of flips, Glenn and Amber still find themselves tempted to make this mistake. However, by experiencing the negative repercussions of using eraser math first hand, they do it a lot less than when they first started. Three common situations where using eraser math can get you in trouble are outlined below:

1. Running the Comps

When you are running the comps on a potential fix and flip and the analysis shows the property will resell for $200,000, don't go back and say "I know the comps show $200,000, but I think I can sell it for $219,000," because you are kidding yourself. At the end of the day, the comps are the comps and that is what the property is probably going to sell for.

2. Project Time

If the average flip time for this property type is 6 months, don't say "I am going to sell it in 3 months." With things like holding costs, interest, taxes, utilities, etc., holding a property for twice as long will result in double the amount of expenses.

3. Hiring Workers

There are many cases where you tell yourself you can cut costs by hiring a cheaper contractor, roofer, manager, etc. upfront. This may make the deal look good on paper, but the potential issues that may arise during the rehab process, like extra management on your part, firing someone half way through, having to hire someone else to redo a job that wasn't done right the first time, and many others may end up costing you more than if you hired the higher quality people up front.

Advice in Action #3: Commit to the following:

- **If the comps tell me a property will sell for $XXX, XXX, then I will move forward as if it is going to sell for that amount. I will not fudge the numbers to force fit a deal.**

- **If a typical project time is X months, then I will move forward as if it is going to take that long or even longer.**

- **I will not just hire someone based on cost alone. I will do my due diligence to make sure I find the highest quality person for the job, even if it is the most expensive.**

If your numbers say the deal will not work, do not fudge the numbers because the only person you are going to fool is yourself.

Advice in Action #4: Ask yourself the following questions:

- **Can you think of a time when you lied to yourself about the details of a deal?**

- **Did the deal end up being successful or unsuccessful?**

- **If you find yourself tempted to fudge the numbers to make a deal work, it probably isn't a deal.**

In the next chapter, you will get two pieces of Best Ever Advice on:

1. A powerful real estate education technique you can implement immediately

2. How to systematize as many aspects of your real estate business and life as possible

CHAPTER 11: SUCCESS SYSTEMS FOR FLIPPERS

"If you want something you've never had, you must be willing to do something you've never done." - Thomas Jefferson

Best Ever Guest: Justin Colby

Justin Colby is the founder of Phoenix Wealth Builders. He is the host of the top ranked podcast "The Science of Flipping" and is the author of "The Science of Flipping."

Episode 64

http://www.thescienceofflipping.com

Justin got started in real estate with a partner in 2007, at the beginning stages of the financial crisis. They always knew they wanted to be fix-and-flip investors. 2007 provided them with an excellent opportunity to capitalize on the sudden influx of foreclosures and short sales. Over the next couple of years, Justin and his partner focused specifically on fix and flips. However, they realized that they were missing many other great real estate opportunities outside of this niche. Starting in 2013, Justin and his partner worked on creating a dynamic real estate business instead of just being a one trick pony.

They were spending a lot of money marketing for deals, but were not capable of taking on every property that came from leads. Instead of passing up on these opportunities, Justin and his partner created a wholesaling division and began wholesaling two to five properties a month, sometimes even more. They have continued flipping, doing over 300 homes over a seven-year period. Justin and his partner are now also beginning to get into development deals.

By working in a wide range of real estate niches, they have picked up great advice and learned valuable lessons that have allowed them to make the transition from fix and flippers to dynamic investors a much easier process. Justin accounts for his business success to investing in a coach, partnering with experienced professionals, focusing on always pushing forward, and systematizing not only their business, but also their lives.

Investing in a Coach

About a year after Justin and his partner started investing, they had completed two deals and made a whopping $14,000 in profit. Since they did not have any other jobs and made $7,000 each for the whole year, they practically went bankrupt. The next year, Justin and his partner decided to invest in coaching. It was the best decision that they ever made. After just two calls with their coach, they went from doing two deals in Year One to doing six deals in Year Two. After even more coaching, they were able to do 20 deals in Year Three.

All Justin and his partner needed was a big brother. They were both smart and educated. Justin had a degree from UCLA and his partner had a degree from San Francisco State. They were hard workers, charismatic, and had everything that they thought they would need to have an easy transition to making a lot more money. After hiring the coach, they realized there were some simple things they needed help with, like organization and most importantly, accountability.

Advice in Action #1: Getting a coach really changed Justin and his partner's business. They thought they knew it all but by simply getting help with organization and having someone to hold them accountable, they were able to take their business to the next level. If you plan on creating a large, successful real estate business, having a mentor, coach, and/or accountability partner is a must.

Education via Partnership

Investing in a coach was a breakthrough moment for Justin and his partner. Organizing their business with the aid of their coach allowed them to quickly scale their business and opened the door to more opportunities in the real estate market. One such opportunity occurred when a friend brought Justin a development deal. At this point, neither Justin nor his partner had any experience in this area. The deal was a piece of land a developer purchased years ago, began putting in the infrastructure (components underground that you do not see when you buying a home), and then went bankrupt. With the majority of the infrastructure installed, Justin knew he was going to be able to save a lot of money. He started doing the math and the price point seemed pretty good. He, therefore, decided to move forward with the deal. Looking back, Justin thinks that this was a bigger risk than he would advise anyone to take, but he felt like they were at a point in their business that the risk was worth the potential payout.

Since Justin and his partner had no prior development education, they hired several consultants to make sure that they were doing it right. They hired bookkeepers, accountants, lawyers, and had people come down from the city to make sure that they were building everything up to code. Partnering with an investor who had development experience is what really allowed Justin to feel confident pulling the trigger on this deal. This partner had already developed over 200 homes. Justin believes that if he weren't able to partner with an experienced and successful developer, it would have been a whole different ball game.

Advice in Action #2: Justin and his partner were able to make up for their lack of education by hiring and partnering with real estate professionals that had years of development experience. It is good to educate yourself on the types of deals you are pursuing, but it is even more important to build a solid team that has experience and past success in what you are looking to accomplish.

Just Keep Pushing

Over the years, Justin learned from his coach and experienced investors that you have to have fortitude in the real estate business. You must be patient and always keep pushing, no matter what. We have all heard the saying "real estate is not a get rich quick" business," so if you are just starting out or waiting for your next big deal, never give up. If you are marketing for deals, keep doing marketing. Be consistent, don't give up, and don't slow down, because this will always result in a deal.

Justin was taught early on that there is no time wasted in real estate. If you are meeting with someone and you are unsure if anything is going to come from it, don't look down on the meeting and think it was a waste of time. You never know when that relationship will re-emerge in the future. You may need them or they may call you with an opportunity years later that will put money in your pocket. Don't get discouraged if you don't have an immediate result right after the meeting.

Advice in Action #3: Remember, there is never any time wasted in real estate. Commit to continuing to meet with real estate professional in all industries, like:

- **Title companies**
- **Loan officers**
- **Brokers**
- **Hard moneylenders**

- Wholesalers
- Fix and flippers
- Property managers
- Appraisers

This also applies to conducting market research, driving around looking at properties, walking through properties, and anything and everything you do that is related to real estate and meeting you goals. Continue taking action and the results will come.

Systematize As Much As Possible

Justin really stresses the importance of creating systems for as many aspects of your business and life as possible. Justin started to see success in his business after deciding to systemize what he and his partner did each and every day. He stopped making excuses for things he didn't or couldn't do, created a daily routine, and committed to never breaking it. Justin compares being an investor to being a shark: you never want to sit still and you always need to be active in order to see huge results. Whether you are looking at a deal, building a buyers list, finding more contractors, or finding more private money lenders, it does not matter. There is always something that you can do. For Justin and his partner, it was the system of building a routine and taking action each and every day that gave them real results and allowed them to create the successful business they have today.

Advice in Action #4: Do you wake up and have a system or routine you follow or do you just get up and wing it? You have seen the power of having a daily routine, so you should want to implement your own system as soon as possible. This is an example of the routine that Justin followed back in 2008 to give you some ideas on the type of process you could create for yourself:

1. Wake up and grab a coffee (Joe would have a big glass of water with wheatgrass)
2. Head to his business partner's home office
3. Commit to 10 phone calls to realtors he had not connected with yet.
   a. Look up realtors on Realtor.com, Zillow, or any of the free sites available
   b. Call and see if they are interested in grabbing a coffee
4. Commit to 10 phone calls to sellers
   a. Look up on Craigslist

Imagine the results you would have if you just called 20 different real estate professionals in a week, let alone each and every single day!

Wrapping up Part Two

In Part Two, you received the Best Ever Fix-and-Flip advice from three successful fix-and-flippers.

In Part Three, you will receive the Best Ever Advice from six successful real estate professionals who utilize hybrid real estate strategies, as well as action items you can immediately implement for your business. To begin, you will get two pieces of Best Ever Advice from an investor on:

1. The lessons learned from one lawsuit-happy tenant
2. Why you need to be intentional in both real estate and life

PART THREE:

THE BEST HYBRID INVESTING MODELS EVER

CHAPTER 12: REAL ESTATE SYNDICATION AND ONE LAWSUIT HAPPY TENANT

"If somebody offers you an amazing opportunity but you are not sure you can do it, say yes – then learn how to do it later." – Richard Branson

Best Ever Guest: Michael Blank

Brief Bio: Michael Blank has put together multiple syndication deals as well as flipped over 30 homes in three years. He also consults investors on apartment investing, raising money, and deal syndication.

Episode 2

http://www.TheMichaelBlank.com

After receiving a Master's Degree in Computer Science, Michael participated in a software start-up and made some capital through an IPO. His initial intentions were to take this capital and start his own software company, but as he began networking with potential entrepreneurs, he didn't really see any opportunity. As Michael began investigating other entrepreneurial options, he came across Robert Kiyosaki's "Rich Dad, Poor Dad." At the time, he was trying to amass a large sum of money in his bank account, but after reading "Rich Dad, Poor Dad," he realize that it wasn't about how much money you have, but how much passive income you are deriving from it.

This made perfect sense. With the combination of not finding opportunities on the software side and the "Rich Dad, Poor Dad" philosophy, Michael decided to pursue franchise restaurants as his cash flow business model. He purchased a territory of pizza restaurants, hired a multiunit restaurant operator to manage the day-to-day operations, funded it himself, and raked in the money.

Restaurants to Real Estate

Michael also learned about the power of real estate investing from "Rich Dad, Poor Dad," so he decided to pursue fix-and-flipping. He did a couple of flips in 2005 and one in 2006. At the same time, Michael was active in apartment buildings. He was doing some marketing in Texas and found a smoking hot deal: an 82-unit complex listed at $1.8 million. Michael put the deal under contract. However, within a few days, he reconsidered. He was extremely busy on the restaurant side, building additional restaurants and buying out other franchisees that wanted to get out of the business, so the prospect of flying to Texas every few weeks became an issue. As a result, Michael backed out of the deal and did not focus much on real estate in 2007 and 2008. His broker actually ended up purchasing the deal and still owns the property to this day.

During Michael's break from real estate, the market tanked, and he was fortunate to have sold all of his properties before this happened. In 2009, his restaurant business was stable enough that he was able to get back into flipping houses. This time around, he wanted to approach it as less of a hobby, and more of a business. At the time, the real estate market was still recovering, so there was an oversupply of foreclosures and the retail market was beginning to improve. This gave Michael the ability to buy inexpensive properties and sell them quickly in the retail market at his target price.

The problem was that he had deployed his net worth into the restaurant business and didn't have any cash left, so he decided to raise money from private investors to fund his deals. He offered investors a 12% interest rate, and required a minimum of $25,000 in capital. Much to his surprise, it was fairly easy to raise private money. Investors understood real estate, enjoyed the 12% return, and were comfortable with the low perceived risk.

Michael knew this type of market was temporary, so he realized he needed to move quickly in order to capitalize. Over the next three years, he successfully flipped 30 properties. After that, the market started to dry up on the acquisition side. There were many buy-and-hold investors who were entering the market, so it became extremely difficult to find deals. Michael also realized that there was nothing passive about flipping houses and decided to pursue commercial real estate.

One Lawsuit Happy Tenant

Michael got back into commercial real estate in 2011. He wanted to get into commercial real estate because it was a better way to build long-term wealth and it gave him the ability to use leverage while creating value. Michael's first experience in commercial real estate was purchasing a 12-unit property in Washington D.C. with a handful of investors. Out of these 12 units, there was one tenant who seemed to have a life mission to bankrupt Michael.

This tenant, let's call him "Jeff," was not only refusing to pay rent, but was calling various government agencies about compliance and enforcement issues. Every other day, Michael had to go to the property to meet with an inspector that "Jeff" had called on. Every time an inspector came, they would find something to write up because if they didn't, they wouldn't have been doing their job. The exposure Michael's building was getting due to "Jeff's" constant claims were very high up in the food chain of the government agencies. As a result, the inspectors were under a lot of pressure to perform, so Michael was facing exceedingly high fines for things that normally aren't enforced. He was under the microscope of agencies involved with construction permits, lead paint, and local associations, among a few others.

On top of the fines, "Jeff" was suing Michael repeatedly for the same violations, so he was going to court every six weeks. He was running up a huge bill because of attorney fees and fines. Since the property was under such scrutiny, he had to pull a permit for everything, even for the small things that aren't normally enforced, like replacing a toilet. The permits needed to be pulled by a licensed electrician, so Michael had to pay $500 just to pull a permit for a $100 toilet. It was difficult on the contractors to have to constantly spend time pulling permits, so many of them quit and Michael had trouble finding replacements.

At one of the court hearings, "Jeff" asked the judge for five minutes to speak with Michael in private. The judge dismissed them and "Jeff" asked if they could grab a cup of coffee after the hearing. After five minutes, they returned to the courtroom. The judge asked how they should proceed, and "Jeff" said that he wanted to drop all charges.

Over coffee, Michael learned that "Jeff" didn't really know the effect he was having. It turns out "Jeff" was really just trying to make sure the city did their jobs more than trying to specifically target Michael. All in all, "Jeff" said "you don't have to worry about me anymore." After his conversation, "Jeff" stopped calling government agencies and moved out shortly after.

Advice in Action #1: As soon as "Jeff" started making life difficult, Michael strongly reconsidered his decision to go into commercial real estate. He was warned about investing in D.C. because of the laws, but even the investors involved in the deal said this situation was new to them. Before you get involved in a new market or new real estate niche, make sure you take the time to research any laws or regulations. This will save you from getting your education the hard way.

The Importance of Due Diligence

Michael learned so many lessons after going through this difficult experience. However, his main takeaway was the importance of performing due diligence on a tenant's history upfront. Michael spoke with a landlord-tenant attorney who advised him to always look up each tenant's court history moving forward. He looked up the tenant's court history after the fact, and discovered that the tenant was in and out of court with his previous landlord too! All Michael had to do was fill out a simple form, which did not take much time at all, especially compared to the time spent dealing with the problem. The more experience someone has with evictions, the more difficult they are going to be. If they have done it before, there is a higher probability they will do it again. In Michael's case, the tenant was very intelligent, determined, and knew how to use the system to their advantage.

Advice in Action #2: At this point, you may be telling yourself "this is a scary story, but it can never happen to me." Michael figured the same thing, but this type of situation can happen to anyone. Commit to not only performing a standard background check on your potential tenants, but take the time to search their court history as well.

Looking back, Michael honestly believes he probably would not have acted any differently. Even if he had discovered the tenant's past court history, he was so eager to do a deal that one issue wouldn't have stopped him from plowing ahead. Michael now understands the potential damage one issue can do and he never overlooks the tenant-landlord history when doing his due diligence.

Advice in Action #3: As an investor, you can look back and question yourself as much as you want. At the end of the day, there is nothing to regret as long as you do the best you can, build in a margin of error, and just take it as it comes. Failure is a part of life and will occur no matter what path you decide to take, so do not let it discourage you. Try to do the best you can!

Be Intentional

Michael's Best Ever advice is to be intentional, in both real estate investing and life in general. Most of the time, we tend to drift through life. Maybe we want a nice house, a million dollars, or to get into real estate investing, but we continue to stay on autopilot. Eventually, we develop a discontent of some sort that starts to grow stronger inside of us. If this discontent becomes strong enough, we start dreaming about what our lives could be like. At this point, we should listen and analyze this inner voice, but we don't do this much. Instead, we normally keep drifting through life and ignore this feeling of discontent.

Advice in Action #4: There are plenty of people who develop a discontent for their job, where they are going in life, or about the size of their retirement account, and dream about what could be. Are you one of these people? Be honest.

If you are intentional, instead of simply fantasizing about what life could be like, you can do something about it. In order to make this decision, you have to consider "why" you actually want to do something about it.

- **Why do you want to change your life?**
- **If you change your life:**
  - What would happen?
  - What would you get?
- **If you don't change your life:**
  - What would be the result?

If you decide to listen to this inner voice and figure why you want change your life, you have to commit to taking action. Let's say you decide to get into real estate investing because you are discontented with your job and where your life is going. You dream about buying a rental property each year for 10 years, so you can retire in 10 years with 10 properties.

It is great that you listened to your inner voice, figured out "why" you want to make a change, and created a plan to make your dream a reality, but you can't skip the most important step. You need to commit to this plan and take the required actions. Many people skip this last step, so they never get started.

After making the commitment and starting to take action, this is when the intentional investor really has to be focused to avoid falling into the shiny object syndrome. You can do wholesaling, rehabbing, lease options, storage units, and much more, but you can't do them all. There are many different niches in real estate, but you have to decide which one you want to pursue.

Advice in Action #5: In the beginning, you have to educate yourself on the different real estate strategies, but at some point, you have to make a decision on what you want to focus on. Select the strategy that works best for what you want to accomplish, stick to it, and master it.

Another common trap new investors fall into is expecting to attain high levels of success in a short window of time. No matter what you do, you need to realize that you will not be successful in 2 months, 6 months, 12 months, or even longer, yet many investors will give up before even making it a year. They don't realize that if they persisted a little longer, they would have gotten over the hump.

Advice in Action #6: The "get rich quick" trap is very difficult to comprehend as a new investor. If you talk to the experienced, successful investors, you will find that it may have taken them several years until they got to the point where they quit their jobs and had a foundation to build on. In order to truly understand, reach out to successful investors in your area and see what they have to say about their experience getting started.

To avoid these traps, be intentional about what you are doing. Get up each and every day and think about what your plans and intentions are. Go back and remind yourself why you decided to invest in real estate and what the rewards will be, and then commit to taking action towards that goal.

In the next chapter, you will get three pieces of Best Ever Advice on:

1. How to find a need in the real estate market, and why you will benefit by filling it
2. A step-by-step hybrid buy-and-hold investment strategy
3. How to benefit from being transparent in your real estate business model

CHAPTER 13: THE HYBRID BUY-AND-HOLD STRATEGY

"There are no secrets to success. It is the result of preparation, hard work, and learning from failure." – Colin Powell

Best Ever Guest: William Robison

William Robison is an experienced real estate broker from Kansas City, Missouri. He also owns and operates a successful property management company.

Episode 09

http://www.kansascityinvestmentrealestate.com

William got started in real estate over ten years ago when he decided to begin flipping properties. While flipping properties, William built many relationships with other investors. As a result, he identified a need for an investor friendly broker who understood the flipping process. He, therefore, obtained his broker's license and began working specifically with these investors. During the economic downturn, William transitioned to working with small banks. He helped them to divest their sudden influx of foreclosed assets. Once the real estate market turned around, William returned to the aspect of real estate that he enjoyed the most, working with investors who were flipping properties.

Find a Need and Fill It

William is a perfect example of someone who identified a need in the market and filled it. He started by flipping properties on his own. However, while networking with other investors, he identified the need for an investor friendly broker. As a result, he obtained his broker's license to fill that need. When the market crashed, instead of giving up on real estate, he identified banks in need of help divesting foreclosed properties and he filled that need.

Advice in Action #1: To start brainstorming potential needs you can fill, the best place to start is with your own business.

Create a list of what you believe to be the 5 most important areas of your real estate business.

1. **Using this list, create a list of 2-3 recurring problems that you are facing in these areas.**

2. **Using this list, brainstorm 2-3 characteristics of an ideal service that would alleviate these problems.**

3. **Select one of these services that most align with your strengths and brainstorm how you can implement this service to add value for your clients.**

What is The Hybrid Buy-and-Hold Strategy?

As a result of flipping properties and working with other investors, William has perfected and transformed his business model into what he calls "The Hybrid Buy-and-Hold Strategy." With a typical "turn-key" model, a broker would have a pipeline of fully rehabbed, rent-ready properties that they would sell to their investor clients. The issue William identified with this model was that investors would have to pay close to full retail for these "turn-key" properties. This was considered to be a good investment, and not a great investment. This was the stimulus for William's "Hybrid Buy-and-Hold Strategy." Instead of helping clients find the end product, which were "turn-key" properties, William and his team assist clients to create the end product through a 4-step process. This process includes: 1) finding a distressed property, 2) overseeing the acquisition process, 3) performing renovations, and 4) leasing and managing the property.

1. Finding a distressed property

William and his team help their clients to find distressed properties. The majority of the properties are foreclosures, but they also look for properties with signs of financial distress (i.e. tax delinquencies, divorce, probate, etc.) and vacancies. The primary goal is to find a property that will have an 85% ARV (after-repair value), meaning that the all-in costs (acquisition + renovations) are 85% of the final property value. This gives the client instant equity in the property through "forced appreciation," which can be used for additional real estate investment opportunities. In the typical "turn-key" model, a client would pay close to retail. Therefore, minimal or no equity is created.

Assume that William finds a foreclosure at a list price of $75,000. He and his team conduct some research and determine that similar, rent-ready properties in the area are selling for $150,000. He also finds that to get the subject property rent-ready will require $50,000 in renovations. After purchasing the property for $75,000 and putting in $50,000 of renovations, William's client has spent a total of $125,000. Since the property is worth $150,000, there is a LTV (loan-to-value ratio) of 83% and $25,000 in equity is created! If the client had used the typical "turn-key" model, they would have paid $150,000 for the exact same property. As a result, they would have missed out on the additional $25,000 in equity, even though both scenarios require a similar amount of effort on their part.

2. The acquisition process

As a broker, William and his team oversee all aspects of the acquisition process, which include the inspection, appraisal, closing procedure,

75,000   purchase
50,000   FMR
125,000

Retal 150,000 turn key
     -125,000
     25,000 equity)
         profit

92

etc. During this process, William will personally visits the property and takes 60 to 80 pictures of the important mechanicals, walls, roof, etc. He tries to include everything that is important and costs money. Based on this visit and the photos, William estimates the rehab costs. He shares this information with his clients so they have an understanding of exactly what they are buying and are able to make an educated decision on whether or not to move forward.

Advice in Action #2: When you are walking through potential properties, take several pictures and videos, following the same process as William. If you are purchasing the property for yourself, these photos will provide a visual reminder of the property's condition, so that you do not have to rely on your memory or the pictures from the property listing.

3. Renovations

Since this is a distressed property situation, the next step after acquisition is to perform the required renovations to get the property rent ready. William and his team will continue to take pictures of the progress and share the photos with their client. Similar to the photos taken during the acquisition phase, the purpose of these photos is to assure the client know that they are getting exactly what they are paying for. If they are expecting granite countertops, then the pictures will show that granite counter tops were installed, and not laminate countertops.

Advice in Action #3: During the different rehab phases, you should continue to take photos, even if you are purchasing the property for yourself. You can use these pictures in combination with the "before" photos to create a project portfolio that you can share with banks or other investors to show your level of professionalism and attention to detail.

4. Leasing & Management

Once the renovations are completed, William's property management team will locate a tenant, go through the leasing process, and then manage the property for their client. This gives William an opportunity to make money on each of these steps. The client, meanwhile, is able to get more value from their purchase than what is typical. Don't you live for win-win scenarios?

Be Proactively Transparent

William believes that it is important to ensure transparency in your business model. This provides a clear understanding of the expectations at the beginning of a project or transaction. Practicing transparency should be applied to all business transactions. By offering information proactively on everything your clients are wondering, you will come out ahead every time. This will tell your clients that you truly care about their experience. It will also enable you to build a higher level of trust. They will definitely know that you are on top of things.

Advice in Action #4: William did not wait for an issue to arise before becoming transparent, because at that point, it would have been too late. He proactively provides his clients with numerous photos so that they always know that he is on top of the situation. You should perform the following exercise to determine how your business can become more transparent:

Which aspects of your business need more transparency? (If you are having trouble coming up with answers, use the list of 5 areas of your business from Action Item #1)

1. **What are some ways you can make these aspects of your business more transparent?**

2. **Commit to taking action on the answers from question 2**

In the next chapter, you will get two pieces of Best Ever Advice on:

1. How to use partnerships to quickly scale your business

2. Lessons learned from losing everything during the financial crash

CHAPTER 14: LESSONS LEARNED FROM LOSING EVERYTHING

"What would you attempt to do if you know you could not fail?" –
Robert Schuller

Best Ever Guest: Kevin Bupp

Kevin Bupp has owned a mortgage company, an event company, and
a printing company. He has been investing for over 14 years and has
done more than $40,000,000 worth of real estate transactions.

Episode 16

http://www.kevinbupp.com

When Kevin was 19 years old, he was introduced to real estate investing
by a local investor, David, who he met through a mutual acquaintance.
David told him what he was doing in real estate, how he spent his spare
time, and provided an overall sense of the lifestyle he lived as a full-time
investor. Kevin was very intrigued.

As a result of Kevin's interest in investing, David invited him to attend a
3-day real estate seminar in Philadelphia. David had already purchased
two tickets, but his business partner couldn't attend, so the timing
could not have been more perfect! At the seminar, Kevin was able to
network with new and experienced investors and also learned how to
invest in single-family residences as a wholesaler and fix-and-flipper.

After leaving the seminar, Kevin was pumped up and excited about the prospect of taking the knowledge he had gained, and using it to get out in the real estate market to make some money.

Learning Through Mentorship

The first item on Kevin's agenda post-seminar was to focus on how to do his first deal, so he reached out to David for advice. Since David had previous experience investing in real estate, he decided to take Kevin under his wing. David wanted Kevin to learn the ins and outs of real estate investing before spending any money so he didn't make any (or as many) mistakes. Kevin literally followed David around for a year, gaining first hand knowledge on what life was like for a full-time real estate investor. Kevin went to his home office every day, and watched what David did, listened to him talk on the phone, went to see properties, and looked at some of the apartments that David owned.

After a year, Kevin decided it was time to pull the trigger and purchase his first property. He found an old, dilapidated property in Harrisburg, PA, purchased it for $26,000 and put in an additional $10,000 in renovations. Kevin funded the project with private money he raised from one of David's investors. He sold the property for $59,000, making a profit of $5,000, which was about as much money he was making in a year working in his current job.

Advice in Action #1: Not only did Kevin learn the ins and outs of real estate investing from his mentor, but he was also able to raise $36,000 in private money from one of his mentor's investors. Gaining knowledge is not the only benefit from having a mentor. If they are active in the market, they will also have a network of other real estate professionals they can send your way. Commit to finding or hiring some sort of mentor and you will benefit in a many of ways.

Scaling Quickly By Starting a Business and Partnering Up

Kevin continued doing fix-and-flips as well as a few wholesale deals on the side while finishing up the last two years of community college in Pennsylvania. Upon graduation, he decided to try his luck in a new market, so he quit his job and moved down to Florida. As soon as he arrived, Kevin started pounding the pavement and got involved in two real estate investing clubs. Through these efforts, he found the good areas of town, determined what he wanted to focus on, and discovered the best way to make money in this new market. It took about 8 months of research and networking before Kevin found his first fix-and-flip deal.

By continuing to fix-and-flip and network, Kevin became familiar with who the active movers and shakers in the market were and what types of investment strategies they were using. Through these experiences, he was able to form two partnerships, both of which allowed him to quickly scale his real estate business.

Partnership #1 – Mortgage Brokerage Firm

One year after making the move to Florida, Kevin partnered up with an entrepreneur who owned a mortgage brokerage firm that already employed 12 full-time loan officers. Together, they originated millions of dollars in loans each month, primarily within the sub-prime niche, and sent out 100,000 pieces of direct mail every month.

Partnership #2 – Investment Group

Kevin had also built a relationship with an experienced investment group in Sarasota. He knew this investment group because he had wholesaled and bought some deals from them in the past. Kevin and this group decided to put their brains together and ended up combining their efforts and partnering up. When Kevin initially met this group, they were doing 10 to 15 deals a month. After the partnership was formed, they were buying 20 properties a month. Their main strategy was long-term buy-and-hold rentals, with the majority of the homes being SFRs, along with a few smaller multifamily properties. By 2007, the partnership had a combined portfolio of 500 SFR rentals. Kevin was not a full partner because this investment group already owned a number of SFRs before he joined, but he was still able to amass a personal portfolio of 100 properties.

Advice in Action #2: Both Kevin and this investment group benefited from partnering up. For Kevin, he was able to scale his business to 100 properties, and the investment group was able to purchase an additional five to ten properties each month. It is extremely difficult to quickly scale a real estate business all alone, so if you plan on building a real estate empire, partnering up with another investor or real estate group is very advantageous. However, make sure that you perform your due diligence up-front, because choosing the wrong partner or entering a partnership at the wrong time can get you into a lot of trouble.

The Effects of The Financial Crisis

Up to this point, everything was going great. Kevin had two successful partnerships and was making a ton of money, but when the market crashed in 2007-08, it started to go downhill fast. First, Kevin sold off his ownership in the mortgage company. This was before the crash was at full force so everything was going okay, but he sold his stake to his partner, who ended up going out of business a year later. Kevin's other partnership was the one that affected him the most.

Leading up to the crash, Kevin and the investment group wanted to mitigate their risk, so they committed to purchase SFR rental properties for no more than 65% of market value. When the financial crisis occurred, not only did property values plummet, but the rental market crashed as well. Homebuilders who had built brand new homes were unable to sell, so they were forced to hold on to them and rent them out.

Unfortunately, these brand new properties were renting for the same price as the 20 to 30 year old homes Kevin and the investment group owned. As a result, they ended up giving 90% of their properties back to the banks.

One would think that someone purchasing properties at 65% of the market value would be able to sustain a crash. However, due to four main factors, this was not the case:

1. *The taxes and insurance rates are much higher in Florida compared to the relatively low rates found in the Midwest.*

2. *Kevin and the investment group had 500 properties, mostly SFRs, spread across 7 different counties that stretched 200 miles north to south, so they had a large property management company with a lot of inefficiencies.*

3. *Many of the markets in Florida had economies revolving around real estate. Once the market crashed, construction workers, real estate agents, and other real estate related employees lost their jobs and their source of income. Kevin and the investment firm were losing tenants and people were leaving Florida faster than they were coming in.*

4. *Property values decreased more than 50%, and in some areas, as much as 65%. Properties they purchased at 65% ARV for $60,000 were selling for $35,000 in 2010.*

The typical home Kevin and the investment group purchased was a 3 bedroom, 1.5 or 2 baths SFR that would cash flow $150 to $200 a month. Even though they were never paying more than 65% ARV plus repairs, after accounting for the four factors above, there was a very small margin to make a profit. A cash flow of $200 per month ($2400 per year) is very easy to lose, if there is turnover. If anything happens, even something as minor as a tenant tearing up the carpet, the repair expense alone would eliminate any profit expected for that year.

Advice in Action #3: Take a look at the four main factors that resulted in Kevin losing 90% of his portfolio and see if any of these apply to your real estate business:

Are you investing in an area with higher than average taxes and insurance rates?

- **Is your portfolio spread across a large region?**

- **Do you know who the main employers are in your market? Does your market have a few large industries or is there a diverse spread of different industries?**

- **When the market crashed, how much did the property values in your market drop?**

If you find that one or more of these factors apply to your business, what can you do to mitigate these risks moving forward?

Looking back, Kevin believes experiencing the market crash was a good thing, although he didn't know this at the time. After giving back 90% of his properties, he spent the next few years licking his wounds. He was stuck in a funk and didn't see the light at the end of the tunnel. Eventually, Kevin took a step back, re-evaluated his life, and instead of being negative and saying "poor me," he decided to put his focus on something else until he was ready to get back into real estate. As a result, Kevin started a few other businesses, a sports apparel company and a printing company, both of which are still running to this day.

Lessons Learned From Losing Everything

As time passed, Kevin began reflecting on his experience of going through the real estate crash and losing everything. He realized he had learned a lot about himself and about real estate investing in general, and figured out what he could have done differently. The answer: investing in cash flow rich properties. Looking back, Kevin wishes he had focused more on multifamily properties and learned many lessons, including:

Invest in multiple larger properties that are closer together. This will spread out your risk and eliminate the inefficiencies of a large property management company. The amount of time and effort it takes to purchase 150 SFRs is also much higher compared to purchasing one 150-unit building with the same type of returns.

- *Out of the 90% of the properties he gave back to the bank, not a single one was a multifamily property. They all survived the crash.*

- *Don't get stuck in your comfort zone. Kevin continued to purchase SFRs because that is what he knew, instead of getting out of his comfort zone and pursuing multifamily investing.*

- *Don't focus on appreciation. Kevin calls appreciation "funny money." It is not spendable unless you sell it at the right time. Don't buy based of the expectation that the market will continue to increase indefinitely, year over year.*

- *Understand your investment criteria before deciding to purchase. Figure out the return on investment you want and commit to only purchasing properties that meet your criteria.*

- *Don't overleverage. Kevin and the investment group would wait until they had 10 to 15 homes. Then they would take a commercial line of credit, pull the money out, and purchase more properties. When the market crashed, they were unable to obtain lines of credit, so everything fell apart.*

Advice in Action #4: The main takeaway is to focus on cash flow. If you are buying for cash flow, you are getting an asset that will continue paying you month after month, no matter what happens with appreciation. Buy for cash flow and have the appreciation be the icing on the cake.

In the next chapter, you will get four pieces of Best Ever Advice on:

1. Techniques to identify value-add opportunities

2. Why you should never underestimate the power of poor management

3. How to make sure that you are always hiring the right person for the job

4. Why you must take a hard look at the truth

CHAPTER 15: TURNING PROBLEMS INTO INCOME

"When someone shows you who they are, believe them the first time." –
Maya Angelou

Best Ever Guest: Jacob Durtschi

Jacob Durtschi is the founder of Jacob Grant Property Management,
which manages residential properties in the Idaho Falls market.

Episode 30

http://www.jacobgrant.com

Jacob got started in real estate over 12 years ago as a multi-family investor in the Idaho Falls market. As a beginning investor, he always looked
for ways to increase profits. However, sometimes he looked in the wrong
places. For example, Jacob would rent out laundry units for $25 per set
and thought he was racking in the cash. He didn't factor in the fact that
every time he installed a laundry set, it took one to two hours, and it
took another one to two hours to take them out. Since Jacob wasn't
paying himself for his time, it seemed as though he was making bank.
However, when he factored in his time investment, he calculated that he
was only making $5 an hour. He was making even less per hour when he
had to perform repairs. Eventually, Jacob hired out the installations and
repairs at $65 per hour. Therefore, after just one repair, all of the profit
was eliminated.

By making additional mistakes during his experience as an investor and managing his own properties, Jacob slowly perfected the skill of not only identifying and solving problems, but also how to turn these problems into profitable endeavors. After 7 years of using this skill to create a profitable investing business, Jacob decided to start his own property management company so he could help other investors also turn problems into profits. Jacob founded Jacob Grant Property Management, which currently manages over 400 properties in Idaho, and is continuing to rapidly expand.

Added Value

Jacob believes that the best way to increase profit is to identify the areas where you can add value. His favorite example of adding value was when he started managing an 84-unit apartment complex that had two onsite laundry facilities. Jacob identified that the laundry units were constantly breaking down and having problems. When these problems came up, he was paying someone $65 per hour to make the repairs. Jacob analyzed the amount of money the laundry facilities were bringing in compared with the amount of money it cost to make the repairs, and he discovered that he was actually losing money.

Jacob began contacting local laundry vendors and found a company that would bring in their own machines and charge the property 50% of the income for renting the machines and any repairs. After removing the old machines and hiring the new laundry vendor, the laundry facilities were running so efficiently that there was no longer a need for the second laundry room. The apartment complex was exclusively one-bedroom and studio units, so Jacob turned the old upstairs laundry room into two studios that each rented for $350 to $400 a month. The costs to convert the laundry room into two studios cost around $20,000, but he was able to increase the rental income by $10,000.

This was a huge value add to the complex and resulted in three major benefits:

1. <u>Decreased expenses</u>

By eliminating the need for the second laundry facility, Jacob was able to decrease the overhead costs, and ultimately turn this expense into income. Instead of paying $65 per hour for repairs, this expense was now covered by 50% of the laundry income and he was able to keep the remaining 50% for himself.

2. <u>Increased income</u>

With the conversion of the old laundry facility into two studio apartments, Jacob was able to increase his rental income by $10,000 a year. Since it cost $20,000 to convert from a laundry room to the two studios, the conversion would pay for itself after only two years. After that, it is an infinite return on investment.

3. <u>Increased property value</u>

The biggest benefit is the increase in property value. For properties 5-units or more, the property value is directly related to the income. Since Jacob was able to increase the income by $10,000, and with a local cap rate close to 8%, the property value increased by about $80,000.

This problem actually was not identified prior to the acquisition of the property. When Jacob took on the property, the owner had the property in his possession for over 5 years. It wasn't until Jacob took over the property, that the problem was identified as a potential value add situation.

Advice in Action #1: Take a look at your properties laundry facilities and see if they are being run efficiently.

- **Do you have too many or too few laundry units?**
- **How often do you have to make repairs? How much are you paying for these repairs?**

- If you have multiple laundry facilities, would it make sense to convert one into additional rental units?

- Take a deep dive into the numbers and see if you can add value by converting the laundry facilities into something more profitable.

The Power of Poor Management

"Never underestimate the power of poor management," says Jacob. As an investor, when you are looking at properties, Jacob says that you have to factor in the costs to turn the property around. Properties that are poorly managed are the ones that are not screening tenants properly, have deferred maintenance, and are not following the basic rules of property management. The costs of getting poor tenants out and turning the property around are typically underestimated, so don't ignore and underestimate these costs.

Advice in Action #2: It is important that you have a detailed picture of how a property is operating before purchasing. Ask to meet with the current property manager or owner, and use the examples from the following list of questions to get the specifics on the property's operations:

- **Why does an application get rejected?**
  - o   See Advice in Action #3, Tenant Screening Process
- **What is your vacancy rate?**
- **What kind of marketing do you have?**
- **What is your fee structure?**

You will need to dig deep into the property management systems because many times, that information is not readily available on the surface.

Jacob learned the power of poor management the hard way when he began managing a 110-unit apartment complex that had been poorly managed for 5 to 10 years. The owner was not onboard to turn the property around or make the necessary investment to get the property to where it needed to be. In the second month of managing the property, Jacob had to evict 8 tenants. The cost of having bad tenants and the lack of owner commitment is underestimated on the front end, and the owner ended up not having the capital required to turn these units around. As a result, the property ended up going back to the bank, which is the worst possible ending.

Advice in Action #3: To avoid these common traps, Jacob recommends keeping an eye out for blatant signs of deferred maintenance during the inspection process and asking the current property manager about their tenant screening process.

<u>Deferred Maintenance</u>

Deferred maintenance typically shows up on the property's exterior first. Ask yourself questions like:

- **How does the yard look?**
- **How does the exterior of the building look? Roof? Siding? Gutters?**
- **Are you seeing any signs of deferred maintenance?**

If you are able to clearly see signs of deferred maintenance, then it is likely there is going to be a lot more that you can't see.

<u>Tenant Screening Process</u>

The simplest way to learn about the current tenant screening process is to ask for an application, fill it out, and see how you are scored. You should then sit down with the property manager and go through the application to see what answers would disqualify a potential tenant. Some examples are listed below, but you can follow a similar process for each application question:

- If I have drug use filled in, would you still be okay with that?

- What if I was dealing drugs?

- What if I had a DUI or DWI?

- How would you deal with someone who got foreclosed on?

You want to look for ambiguities. These are some examples of potential red flags you may come across:

- They cannot provide you with specifics on disqualifications.

- They do not follow a system at all.

- Their system is to speak with people on the phone and just get a feel for it.

You should also ask to see the delinquency report. If they do not have one or they have high delinquency rates, it is a sign that they do not have tenants that are easy to manage.

Hire the Right People for the Job

Jacob finds that when issues or problems arise, the property and owner managers will often do everything they can to save a buck by hiring someone for the job who is the cheapest option. For example, if he has a plumbing issue, he has the option to hire a handy man for $35 per hour or a plumber for $65 per hour. Jacob will almost always hire the plumber. He has found that many property managers will hire the handyman. However, the handyman ends up taking a lot longer to fix the problem. When you look at the numbers, you end up not really saving any money because of how long it took. The handyman may also not have fixed it right and you'll have to pay someone else to fix it again. The moral of the story is that the cheaper option may end up costing you more in the long run.

Jacobs believes there is nothing wrong with going with the cheaper option in certain situations, but it becomes a problem when trying to save money is a tendency. As owners, we are always trying to save money and cut costs. However, it is important to take a look at the hard truth to see if there is truly a saving. Sometimes it is as simple as hiring an electrician for an electrical problem, but problems are typically unique and not so black and white. For example, what if you have water in your basement? Who do you hire, a handyman, a plumber, or maybe even a flood specialist? Jacob says that it is very important to look at the results and adjust from there. If you hire the handyman and he ends up not being able to get the job done, then you will know that next time a similar issue arises, you will need to hire a plumber or a flood specialist.

Advice in Action #4: When you are hiring someone to fix maintenance issues, make sure that you are analyzing the actual results on an ongoing basis. Here are some of the items you should be looking at:

- **Actual costs vs. quoted or expected costs**
- **Actual repair time vs. quoted or expected repair time**
- **Quality of work**
- **Was the job done right the first time?**

Feel free to add any additional items to this list and use this list to create your own evaluation process. You should not just assume that you are hiring the right person for the job. You need to have an ongoing process that allows you to know what the real numbers are behind each of your decisions, so you can make the optimal adjustments moving forward.

Take a Hard Look at the Truth

Jacob's last piece of advice is to always "take a hard look at the truth," which applies to all the pieces of advice given above. For his laundry situation, he was kidding himself when he was saying that he was making money on those laundry units. Jacob was able to figure out that he was actually losing money, but only after taking a hard look at the truth.

Advice in Action #5: Just like Jacob and his laundry example, every manager and owner has their own hard truths that they should be looking at. Do not be afraid by what you might find. Taking a look at these hard truths will uncover opportunities for you to make adjustments and ultimately increase your bottom line.

Jacob finds that many newer investors will get super excited when they are looking at potential properties to buy. This excitement can be a positive, but he commonly see that it ends up putting the blinders on and they may miss potential problem areas. Jacob also sees people become complacent with their systems and do not constantly work to improve. Both of these examples are a result of not taking a hard look at the truth.

In the next chapter, you will get the Best Ever Advice on:

1. The most overlooked expenses by buy-and-hold and fix-and-flip investors

CHAPTER 16: COMMONLY OVERLOOKED EXPENSES

"Don't worry about failure, you only have to be right once." –
Drew Houston

Best Ever Guest: Mark Ferguson

Mark Ferguson is the founder of "Invest Four More," a real estate
investing blog. He is a real estate agent and runs a team of 10 that
has sold, on average, 200 homes a year for the last 4 years. Mark is an
active real estate investor, owning 16 investment properties. He fix and
flips between 10 and 15 properties a year.

Episode 57

http://www.investfourmore.com

Mark was exposed to real estate at a very young age. His father was a real
estate agent and also did fix and flips. As a result, Mark got started in real
estate by helping his father with flips during high school. Having been
exposed to real estate at such an early age, Mark told himself that he
would never get into the real estate industry. Instead, he went to college
and obtained a degree in business finance. After graduating, Mark could
not find a job in the world of business finance, so he decided he would
do real estate part-time, only until he found a job. In 2001, Mark re-en-
tered real estate as an agent, and struggled for a long time. He did not
have a niche, he didn't have any goals, and he wasn't great at talking to

people. This all changed when Mark found the REO foreclosure niche. He started listing REOs, started making goals, and his career took off.

In 2010, Mark began investing in single-family rentals, purchasing 16 properties over the next 5 years. In 2013, Mark took over his father's existing fix-and-flip business and real estate sales team. He has been focusing on that business as much as possible. If being a real estate agent, a buy-and-hold investor, and a fix-and-flipper wasn't enough, Mark also started a real estate blog, "Invest Four More," where he writes articles about his past and current experience as an agent and investor.

Real Estate is Very Region Specific

Mark's real estate agent, buy-and-hold, and fix-and-flip business models focus on single-family residences in the Denver area. Within the Denver area, Mark's target sub-market is 50 miles north of the city. In this area, prices are more reasonable and he can acquire a property between $80,000 and $150,000. The reason why Mark focuses on single-family instead of multifamily properties is two-fold:

1. *Since he focuses on SFR as a realtor, he knows the properties very well, so he can get a much better deal and make more money on a SFR compared to a multifamily*

2. *Real estate is very region specific. He pays considerable attention to different parts of the country and the different terms that people get. For whatever reason, Colorado has horrible cap rates compared to other parts of the country. It is hard to find any multifamily properties above a 5% cap rate.*

Due to these two reasons, Mark can be much more successful with SFRs than he can with multifamily in his specific market. He focuses on buying below market value through short sales, REOs, estate sales, etc., so he can make money as soon as he buys the property.

Overlooked Expenses: Buy and Holds

Rents have shot up in Mark's market over the last couple of years. As a result, he can purchase a SFR for around $120,000 to $140,000 that will rent for $1,500 a month. If he were to purchase a multifamily property, he could get a 4-unit with 2 beds and 1 bath per unit for $250,000 that might rent for $2,000 a month. Compared to most parts of the country, this is backwards, but again, real estate is very region specific.

When investing in SFR rentals, Mark strongly advises that you invest for cash flow. Many people get caught up in a rising market and just buy any investment property they can find. However, they neglect to take a closer look at the actual numbers and operations. People get in trouble because they think that if the property rents for $1000 a month and their fixed expenses (mortgage, taxes, and insurance) are $500 a month, then they will cash flow $500 a month. They factored in the fixed expenses but they overlooked additional expenses, like vacancies and maintenance. If the market goes down and they cannot maintain the $1000 a month in rent, then they have properties that are not making money and they cannot sell, so they are stuck. When you invest for cash flow and figure in all of the additional expenses, if the market goes down, you will still make money and can weather the storm.

Advice in Action #1: When investing for cash flow, make sure that you are figuring in vacancy and maintenance costs on top of your mortgage, taxes and insurance:

- **Vacancy**
    - Expect at least a 5-10% vacancy rate, even if the historical rates are much lower
    - One eviction or bad tenant can create that 10% pretty quickly

- **Maintenance:**
    - o A little harder to estimate because it varies depending on the property's condition, age, and how good your tenants are
    - o Figure at least 10%, but more often 15-20% for maintenance and capital expenditures
    - o If you need to replace a roof, these costs can add up pretty quickly

These rates are a percentage of the properties gross rent. If your gross rent is $1,000 per month, figure in $50 to $100 a month for vacancy and $150 to $200 a month for maintenance.

Overlooked Expenses: Fix and Flips

On the fix and flip side, Mark can purchase a property for $80,000, put in an additional $15,000 to $20,000 in renovations, and sell it for $140,000 to $150,000. Being all-in at $100,000 and selling for $150,000, one would think that the net profit is $50,000. However, in reality, this is not the case. After factoring in holding costs, carrying costs, financing costs, and all the other costs that many people do not consider, the profit is closer to $25,000.

As a fix and flipper, you have to understand your actual costs. In Mark's example above, if he overlooked the additional expenses, he would have expected a $50,000 profit instead of the actual $25,000. If the numbers were even tighter and he expected a $20,000 to $25,000 profit, he would have ended up breaking even or potentially even losing money on the deal.

Advice in Action #2: When performing a fix and flip, make sure you figure in the additional expenses on top of the rehab budget. These expenses include:

- **Holding Costs**
- **Financing Costs**
- **Insurance**
- **Utilities**
- **Maintenance**
- **Everything else that goes on during the course of a flip**

Most experienced fix and flippers account for most of these additional expenses, but Mark finds two other surprising costs that many flippers still overlook:

1. Higher Than Expected Repair Costs - Mark has been fix and flipping properties for a long time, and every single time, the repairs end up being higher than expected. You don't really know how much work a house needs until you start getting into it and really have a contractor take a look at what is there. There are always hidden surprises, especially on larger renovations and when you are knocking down walls.

Advice in Action #3: To account for these surprise costs, Mark always adds at least $5,000 to his repair budget automatically. On a $20,000 rehab, that is an additional 25%. Commit to doing the same.

2. Longer Than Expected Project Time – Similar to Mark's experience with the repair costs always being higher than expected, the same holds true for the project time. The length of time it takes to flip a property is almost always longer. There is a huge difference in holding costs if the project time is 4 months vs. 6 months. That extra time can result in up to $10,000 in additional expenses.

Advice in Action #4: Mark always tacks on an additional two months to his expected project time, and adjusts his holding costs accordingly. Commit to doing the same.

In the next chapter, you will get two pieces of Best Ever Advice on:

1. How to use a quick two-step evaluation process on a potential investment property to determine if further analysis is warranted

2. House hacking, a step-by-step strategy for newbie investors to build a real estate portfolio

CHAPTER 17: HOUSE HACKING

"The harder I work, the luckier I get." – Samuel Goldwyn

Best Ever Guest: Brandon Turner

Brandon Turner is the co-host of the popular BiggerPockets podcast with Joshua Dorkin. He is actively involved in writing in-depth real estate articles for BiggerPockets and other online business platforms.

Episode 82

http://www.biggerpockets.com

Brandon got started in real estate when he was 21 years, doing a live-in flip. He purchased a property, moved in, fixed it up, sold it, and made a little bit of money. This was all before the real estate crash. Brandon's next investment was a duplex, where he lived in one unit and rented out the other. The mortgage payment was $620 a month and Brandon rented out the other unit for $650 a month, so he was able to live for free. At this point, the passive income rental thing was becoming pretty cool!

Brandon continued to collect more rental units, started doing a little flipping and land-lording, and kept building up his buy-and-hold portfolio. He is not living in the properties anymore, but he still likes the smaller 2 to 4 unit properties. In his area, these types of properties cash flow really well. Brandon also has a 24-unit property and loves it.

Moving forward, he would like to start buying larger properties and do syndications on apartment complexes as well.

Quick Evaluation Process

When Brandon is evaluating a potential deal, he uses a quick two-step evaluation process to determine if further analysis is worth pursuing. He first filters based off the location, and then utilizes the 50% rule.

1. Location

Brandon will not look at a property if it is in a location that he or his wife does not feel comfortable going to. His wife does most of the property management, so if she is needed at the property, Brandon wants to make sure she feels safe and comfortable.

Advice in Action #1: It is important to budget for property management when you are analyzing a potential investment, even if you plan on managing the property yourself. This will allow you to easily hand off the property to a management company in the future. If you do not budget for property management at the start, your cash flow will take a hit when that day finally comes.

2. The 50% Rule

The 50% rule is a rule of thumb that allows you to quickly screen a potential investment. This rule assumes that 50% of whatever comes in as income will go out in expenses, excluding the mortgage payment. For example, if you apply the 50% rule to a 4-unit property that rents for $500 per unit for a total of $2,000 in income per month, your remaining cash flow will be $1,000 per month minus your mortgage payment. For Brandon, if he applies the 50% rule and there is $100 per month in cash flow, he will pursue it further, dig in, and perform a more detailed analysis.

To determine the accuracy of the 50% rule, Brandon sat down and analyzed his properties using the actual expenses. For his 24-unit property, the expense ratio came out to 55%. He doesn't use a property management company, so the expenses would have been closer to 62-63%. For a triplex, Brandon calculated the expense ratio to be less than 40%. Each tenant in this triplex pays their own water, sewer, and garage, so it is a unique situation where Brandon pays very few expenses.

Advice in Action #2: The 50% rule is just a quick, rule of thumb tool you can use to quickly screen a property. The expenses include vacancy, repairs, capital expenditures, reserves, taxes, insurance, etc. 50% typically works pretty well, but sometimes 60% or 40% end up being more accurate. Do not buy based off of this rule alone! It is just a quick first pass test to see if further analysis is worth pursuing.

House Hacking

Brandon believes investors who are just getting started should seriously consider house hacking. Everyone has to live somewhere, and if you are living in a property you own, it is more than likely a liability, not an asset. If you can combine where you live with an investment property, you get two deals out of one. This strategy is what Brandon calls house hacking. One way you can house hack is to purchase a single-family property with the assumption that you will add-value to force appreciation so you can make a profit when you sell it. An even better strategy is to purchase a 2 to 4 unit multifamily, live in one unit, and rent out the others. Using this strategy, you have the opportunity to live for free or make a small profit. You also get to learn how to be a landlord.

Advice in Action #3: House hacking does not necessarily mean you have to purchase a multifamily. However, if you are buying a property, look at it as an investment regardless.

The first step to house hacking is speaking with a bank to see what it takes to qualify for a residential owner-occupied loan. These types of loans are easier to get, but there are still rules that you have to follow. If the bank requires a 625 credit score and you have a 525, figure out what you need to do to add 100 point to your score. If you need to make $3,000 a month and you are only at $2,200, find out how you can make an additional $800. Typically, you can obtain an FHA loan, which is a first-time homebuyer loan that is 3.5% down. If you are house hacking a $100,000 property, it is only $3,500 out of pocket!

The second step to house hacking is to remember that it is no good to you if you do not buy a good enough deal. Since you are obtaining an owner-occupied loan, your payment is going to be just as high as if you were going to buy a personal house. Understand how to do the math and analyze a deal to make sure you get a good return on your time and your money. House hacking will not turn a bad deal into a good deal.

Advice in Action #4: For FHA loans, the bank typically requires that you live there for at least 1 year. After the year is up, you do not have to refinance the property. You can just move out, put a renter in, and keep the same loan. If you want to obtain another FHA loan for another house hack, you are only allowed to have one FHA loan at a time (except for a couple of exceptions). You will have to either sell the property or refinance to a conventional mortgage if you want to house hack again.

Loans that are less than 20% down also likely require private mortgage insurance (PMI). Make sure that you keep this in mind when you are analyzing a potential house hacking situation. Once you believe you have obtained 20% financing, reach out to your bank for an appraisal to see if you can eliminate the PMI.

Wrapping up Part Three

In Part Three, you received Best Ever Advice from six successful real estate professionals who utilize hybrid investment strategies including:

In Part Four, you will receive Best Ever Advice from two successful property management experts, as well as action items you can immediately implement for your buy-and-hold or property management business. To begin, you will get two pieces of Best Ever Advice on:

1. How to find the right property management company to optimize your property's operations

2. How you can add value by simply reworking your property's existing operating budget

PART FOUR:

THE BEST PROPERTY MANAGEMENT ADVICE EVER

CHAPTER 18: SLASH EXPENSES, MAKE MONEY

"Never complain and never explain" – *Benjamin Disraeli*

Best Ever Guest: Amy Bors

Amy Bors is the founder of Winfield Property Management. She is also the President of both the Tulsa Apartment Association and the Oklahoma State Apartment Association.

Episode 37

http://www.winfieldliving.com

Amy got started in real estate back in 1997, when she took a job with a national management company. She traveled all over the United States performing start-up projects on large distressed multifamily properties. Eventually, Amy decided to start her own management company. Her job required extensive travel and she had a child at home, so she wanted to stay closer to home. She also identified a large need in her local market, Tulsa, for a hands-on management company, which is what she had been doing for almost 10 years. As a result, Amy founded Winfield Property Management in 2006.

With Winfield Property Management, Amy and her team continued to focus on start-up projects on distressed properties in B and C class neighborhoods. They find value-added opportunities where properties require a significant amount of rehab work, purchase with all cash, and hire out an entire crew to perform the renovations. Once the properties are rent-ready, they fill the properties with tenants, refinance, and take their funds on to the next deal. The projects usually take a total of 12 to 24 months.

Find the Right Management

At Winfield Property Management, Amy and her team also work with out-of-state investors who are looking for someone to manage and take care of their properties at the local level. They find their clients a distressed or mismanaged property and add value by reworking the budget and individual units. If an out-of-state investor reaches out to Amy and is interested in an investment that is not her company's specialty, she recommends that they contact a management company that specializes in that specific investment type.

Amy sees many management companies take on projects they do not specialize in, and it just does not work. As a result, she believes it is very important to take the time to find a management company that has the expertise in the type of property you are investing in. If you are investing in an A class neighborhood, reach out to a management company that specializes in A class neighborhoods. If you are investing in student housing, reach out to a management company that specializes in student housing. Amy only takes on properties that fall into her company's specialty, and passes on anything else.

Advice in Action #1: To optimize your properties operations, make sure the management company that you hire specializes in your specific investment style.

Reworking the Budget

Amy and her team add value to properties through rehabs, but also by reworking the operating budget. The overall goal is to achieve a 50 to 55% expense ratio when the property is operating at 95% occupancy. She has seen that properties with expense ratios of 60 to 65% are very difficult to manage effectively, so achieving 50 to 55% is extremely important. To achieve this expense ratio, Amy and her team go through the budget, line by line, to see where improvements can be made. The three main areas that Amy and her team have found where you can really slash costs are the layout of the staff, payroll, and ongoing maintenance.

1. Layout of Staff

Office Staff –Amy's rule of thumb is having 1 office staff member for every 100 units. For example, she has a 364-unit apartment complex that has 3 solid office staff members, which functions very well. At one point, Amy tried adding a 4th member and found that the office cannot function efficiently with another person.

Maintenance Staff – The number of maintenance staff members depends on the type of property. Most of the properties that Amy manages were built between 1968 and 1985 and require considerable maintenance. As a rule of thumb, she likes to have 1 or 2 maintenance staff members for every 100 units.

Advice in Action #2: Keep in mind that if you are finding inefficiencies in your management or operations, adding additional staff members may not be the right solution. You may find that you have too many staff members or it is something else entirely.

2. Payroll

Office Payroll – For leasing agents, expect to pay between $10 to $15 per hour and $30,000 to $60,000 a year for office managers. The additional cost of staffing extra managers or leasing agents can be significant.

Maintenance Payroll – Amy has maintenance rates ranging from $10 per hour for a handyman, and up to $22 per hour for licensed HVAC, plumbing, or electrical specialists, with groundskeepers, painters, maintenance technicians, and others in the middle. Amy likes to keep as much maintenance in house as possible and have full-time maintenance staff that can perform a wide range of tasks.

It is important to note that geography is also a factor when estimating compensation (i.e. a NYC manager will get paid more than someone in Brownsville, Texas)

Advice in Action #3: A painter can do more than just paint inside homes, just like a plumber can do more than just unclog toilets. When hiring maintenance staff members, try to find someone who can wear multiple hats.

3.   Ongoing Maintenance

Amy believes people undervalue going back to your vendors and insurance carriers every year to see where costs can be reduced. For example, Amy was able to negotiate with a landscaping vendor for a price decrease from $2,500 to $2,200 per month. That is a savings of $3,600 a year for each property. These little expense cuts can add up quickly. For example, if the cap rate is 8%, then this savings increases the value of the property by $45,000 ($3,600 / 8% = $45,000)

Advice in Action #4: Make sure you are going back to ALL of your vendors every year to negotiate the best pricing. You can also shop around with other vendors to see if you can find the same quality service for a better price.

In the next chapter, you will get two pieces of Best Ever Advice on:

1.   How you can pull together and share content using information you are already learning yourself

2.   Why you should be automating your entire land-lording process

CHAPTER 19: NEVER RECEIVE A LATE PAYMENT FROM A TENANT

"You are what you eat. You are what you consume." – Lucas Hall

Best Ever Guest: Lucas Hall

Lucas Hall is the Chief Landlordologist at Cozy, which provides free rental management software to landlords. He is also the founder of Landlordology.com, which has extensive information on the landlord-tenant laws in all 50 states.

Episode 73

https://cozy.co/

Lucas got started in real estate because he was trying to impress a girl. He knew her through a weekly event that he attended. One week, he built up the courage to walk up to her and say "what'd you do this week?" She said the bought a house and was in the process of finding people on Craigslist to live with her so she could basically live for free. Lucas thought her idea (and her) were ingenious, smart, and pretty.

Since Lucas had a crush on her, he reached out to her sister, a real estate agent, and asked her to find a bigger house in the same neighborhood. Lucas found a house that was six or seven blocks away and did the same thing his crush did, found renters to live with him so he too could have his mortgage covered and live for free. Shortly after making this purchase, Lucas and his crush started dating, and flashing forward to the present time, they have been married for over seven years.

The Best Landlord Online Resource on the Planet

This purchase launched him on his career as a landlord. For many years, he was an IT consultant for the federal government, so he was flustered by the lack of technological resources dedicated to teaching independent landlords how to manage properly, effectively, and efficiently. After having about six years of landlord experience under his belt, Lucas had gotten it down to a science where it was not only easier, but also very profitable. All of his friends were coming to him asking him questions about being a landlord anyway, so he decided to just take what he learned and make it available online.

The act of making this information available online is what started Landlordology.com. Lucas had a web background from his time as an IT consultant, so he was confident that he could develop the best online resource for landlords on the planet. One and a half years after starting this project, Lucas was approached by Cozy. They said they had been watching him, loved what he was doing, and wanted to acquire Landlordology.com to make it part of the Cozy portfolio. Cozy got their seed money from Google so they had some large backers. They were interested in doing the same thing as Lucas, which was educating landlords. However, Cozy was doing it through software while Lucas was doing it with articles, tips, advice, and guides. Lucas agreed to join Cozy, where he is currently the Chief Landlordologist. He manages Landlordology.com and is also working with Cozy to develop the best online software that landlords and property managers can use to collect rent, screen tenants, list properties, and streamline their business.

Advice in Action #1: Lucas was already educating himself and creating content to improve his landlord business, so it was simple to just

upload that information online and share it with friends and other landlords. Since you are also already learning yourself, why not share this same information with others? Using the follow examples, you should be able to pull together short, useful tips or long in-depth articles and then continue researching the other things that you do not know.

- **Reading**
    - o Lucas has read every book on "landlords" that he could find.

- **Experience**
    - o Lucas used his 10 years of landlord experience, where he has handled almost every possible situation.

- **Lessons learned from successes and failures**
    - o With 10 years of experience, Lucas has learned many lessons on what to do and what not to do.

Automate Your Process

Lucas believes that if you want to be a successful landlord, the best thing that you can do is automate your processes. You should be efficient and try to find inexpensive processes to make things go smoother. The one automated process Lucas implemented that change his life drastically as a landlord is when he started collecting rent online. He now makes online rent collection mandatory for all his tenants. Ever since he started doing this five years ago, he has never had a single late payment. Creating automated processes lets you free up your time so you can focus the majority of your time growing your business, instead of on the monotonous day-to-day activities.

Advice in Action #2: With the abundance of software available, you have the capacity to automate almost every single real estate activity that your business does.

- **Rental Listings**
  - o Instead of posting listings or having someone do it for you
  - o Use a tool like Cozy and Zillow Rental Manager, where you can create a single ad and have it sent out to every major listing site

- **Rental Applications**
  - o Instead of using paper applications, use online applications

- **Rent Collection**
  - o Instead of collecting rent in person, start collecting rent automatically
  - o You can use an online rental collection service like Cozy, or at the very least, have your tenants login to their bank's website and set up an automatic mailer to have their rent mailed automatically each month

- **Lease Signing**
  - o Instead of signing leases in person, use e-signatures or digital signing
  - o Resources you can use are Hellosign.com or Cudasign. com

Wrapping up Part Four

In Part Four, you received Best Ever Advice from two property management experts who implement successful property management strategies.

In Part Five, you will receive Best Ever Advice from two successful lenders, as well as action items you can immediately implement for any real estate investment business. To begin, you will get three pieces of Best Ever Advice on:

1. Why you should build a relationship with a lender from the beginning, even before you start looking at properties

2. How a lender will evaluate your multifamily loan application and what you need to do to make sure that you get approved

3. How to invest in real estate when you don't have a job or prior experience

PART FIVE:

THE BEST LENDING ADVICE EVER

CHAPTER 20: THE INVESTOR-LENDER RELATIONSHIP

"Git er done!" – Larry the Cable Guy

Best Ever Guest: Paul Peebles

Paul Peebles has over 30 years of experience in arranging commercial financing for borrowers and institutional clients. He has closed on over $1 billion in real estate transactions. He is currently a national underwriter and principal at Old Capital Lending

Episode 45

http://www.oldcapitallending.com

Paul got started in real estate 30 years ago as a lender. He worked for the largest institutions in the US and picked up great information on how to structure real estate transactions. For the past 10 years, Paul has been an underwriter for Old Capital Lending, focusing mostly on apartment lending in the Dallas-Fort Worth, Austin, and San Antonio markets. Within in the apartment-lending niche, Paul specializes in structuring transactions for B and C class apartment complexes. Prior to 2015, he had closed on over 4,000 commercial real estate loans. In 2015, Old Capital Lending closed over $300 million, with 1 out of every 3 loans for B and C class apartment complexes in North Texas. Having 30 years of active lending experience, Paul can provide a banker's perspective on what they like to see from investors who are looking to qualify for a loan, especially for investors with little or no experience.

Build a Relationship

When you are purchasing a property with a bank loan, you are signing up for a partnership with that bank. This "partnership" is typically structured with the real estate investor putting up 25 to 30% of the funds and the bank bringing the remaining 70 to 75% of the funds. Just like any partnership, whether it is a marriage, friendship, business partner, etc., you wouldn't just go all in without building some sort of relationship first. Therefore, the same logic applies for relationships with banks.

Build a relationship with your lender from the beginning, even before you start looking at properties. Paul has seen many first time investors make the mistake of assuming they can pursue a property first and worry about finding a bank later. Sometimes it works out and you can get the loan, but Paul typically sees investors run into problems, especially when it comes to obtaining a loan on an apartment complex or in other unique niches. After running into issues on the first property, he finds that for the next deal, investors will always contact the bank on the front end to make sure they are on board.

Advice in Action #1: If you are a brand new investor and do not have a relationship with a lender, commit to building one as the first step. This person can be a banker, mortgage broker, or anyone that has expertise in the field you are looking to pursue.

There are many banks out there, both community and national, who say they can do apartment or unique lending. However, when there is a deal on the table, they cannot follow through if it is not in their wheelhouse. For example, if you are looking to invest in a B or C class apartment complex in Dallas, you will find that there are over 1600 banks in the entire state of Texas, half of which are located in the Dallas area. Out of these 800 banks, about 200 to 300 will provide real estate lending in general. Out for these 200 to 300 banks, not all of them want to do apartment lending or B and C class property types. Since Paul's market is Dallas, he estimates that there are around 10 to 12 banks who are lending on these types of value-add apartment complexes. This is why it is important to not only build a relationship with a bank first, but to make sure that you seek out the right bank. In the Dallas example, you only have 10 to 12 banks to choose from. If you find an apartment complex before building a relationship with one of these 10 to 12 banks, you will discover that the majority of the banks you approach will reject your loan application. As a result, you may end up losing the deal. Even worse, you may get the property under contract, pay for inspections, appraisals, etc., and then have the bank tell you, "You know, I don't think we do this type of loan."

Advice in Action #2: Whether you already have a relationship with a lender or not, before aggressively pursuing a potential investment, reach out to banks to make sure they provide loans for that specific type of property. This applies to most, if not all, situations, including:

- **Brand new investors who are just getting started**
- **Seasoned investors who are looking to expand to a new market location**
- **Seasoned investors who are looking to expand to a new property type**
- **Other types of investors**

If you are a brand new to apartment complexes, Paul advises you to be patient and to take it one step at a time. When you are building a relationship with a lender, find someone who has done apartment loans in the past. They can walk you through your first transaction and lay out the exact steps you need to take. Paul sees many people who have not done an apartment complex deal who go to a random local bank to get a loan. However, you really want to find an expert. Since investing is based on cash-flow, and there is a big different between getting a 15 to

20-year loan from a local bank and a 25 or 30-year loan from a bank that specializes in apartment loans. With the 15 or 20 year loan, you will be paying down the mortgage faster and reduce the bank's risk, but you are not going to be putting as much money in your pocket due to a higher monthly mortgage payment.

Advice in Action #3: One way to gain experience on apartment complexes or real estate investing, in general, is through the guidance of a bank as outlined above. Another way is by listening to real estate podcasts. Real estate podcasts are a great way to quickly learn from many different active and successful real estate investors. If you come across an episode with a guest that is already successful in the niche that you are interested in pursuing, reach out to them and tell them what you are looking to do. You never know where the relationship may go.

The Structure of Real Estate Transactions

When Paul is evaluating a loan application, two-thirds of the lending decision is based on the collateral itself (the property). The types of items he looks at for a property are the following:

- *Past and present performance*
- *Location*
- *Tenant base*
- *Demographics*
- *All bills paid or individually metered*
- *Roof type and condition*
- *Your plan for what you are going to do after you buy the property, like a rehab*
- *Monthly pro forma*

The other one-third of the decision is based on the borrower. The types of items he looks at for a borrower are the following:

- *Personal financial statements*
- *Liquidity*
- *Credit*
- *Tax returns*
- *Experience*

Advice in Action #4: Now that you have an idea of what a lender is looking for, make sure you are doing your due diligence on both the property and yourself ahead of time. By proactively obtaining this information, you can save both your time and the banks' time. As a result, you will look much more professional in the eyes of the lender.

Don't Have a Job or Experience?

Paul has done many deals with investors that do not have an income, job, or experience, but do have liquidity. If you have liquidity, it cures a lot of sins. When Paul says liquidity, it is not the same as equity.

- Liquidity

Liquidity is money you can access in a few days. Examples of liquidity are cash, stocks, and bonds.

- Equity

Equity is money you cannot access quickly. Examples of equity are the difference between a home's value and how much is owed, a 401k, an IRA, and an annuity.

Paul has general guidelines and terms for investors that come to him looking to buy a multifamily property, but lack experience and/or have no job. As an example, let's say you are looking to buy a property for

$900,000 and it requires $100,000 in renovations, so your all in price is $1 million. First off, you will want to find a lender who will include the renovation costs in the loan so you do not have to come up with an additional $100,000. Paul provides these types of loans all the time.

With an all-in price of $1 million, you may need to come up with 30% for the down payment. You will bring $300,000 to closing and Paul will bring the remaining $700,000. At this point, you are not out of the water yet, because Paul wants to see "post-equity liquidity." This type of liquidity is how much money you have left over for a rainy day. If a problem arises after closing, like an insurance claim, the rehab doesn't take, or you cannot fill the building with tenants, Paul will turn to you to cover these expenses. Therefore, on top of the 30% down payment, Paul wants to see an additional 25-30% of the loan amount in liquidity. This will ensure that if the property needs a new parking lot, the chiller system has gone down, or any other issue arises, you can write a check to cover the expense.

Advice in Action #5: When you are analyzing multifamily deals, make sure that you are accounting for the 25-30% post-equity liquidity on top of the down payment and other closing costs.

If you do not have a job or have no experience, whether you have liquidity personally or not, you are still able to qualify for a loan, as long as somebody on your team has a job, experience, and the required liquidity. This situation is known as syndication. As a syndicator, you would be the managing partner. You would be the boots on the ground that is responsible for finding the property, talking with the listing agent, and getting the property under contract. A syndicator may have no or some money, so they are looking for other partners that will put money into the deal. These other partners are guarantors in the transaction. As long as you can come up with the required liquidity for the deal between yourself and other partners, the deal can move forward.

For example, Paul did a deal with a syndicator in Austin, TX who did not have a job. The syndicator had $200,000 in liquidity and needed to

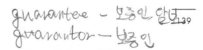

raise an additional $750,000 to cover the down payment and post-equity liquidity requirement. The syndicator raised $750,000 from two other people, and all three had to sign the mortgage note. Paul closed the deal with a 30-year amortized loan with a 5-year term at an interest rate just under 4%. By raising the extra $750,000 in capital and having 2 employed partners sign the note, the syndicator was able to close the deal, even without a job.

Advice in Action #6: Just because you do not have a job or the money to fund a deal does not mean you have to walk away. As a real estate investor, it is your job to find creative ways to structure deals, and acting as a syndicator is a great way to get into very large deals that you would not be able to purchase on your own.

To learn more about syndication, subscribe to the "Joe Fairless – Best Real Estate Investing Advice Ever Show" channel on YouTube, where Joe gives weekly tips on how to raise money and buy apartment communities.

One final note: When investing in multifamily properties, the lending is different from residential lending. In residential lending, if you don't have a job or if you have too many home loans, you get penalized.

In the next chapter, you will get two pieces of Best Ever Advice on:

1. Why you need to have a long-term real estate approach
2. The four questions multifamily brokers have when qualifying investors, and what your answers need to be

CHAPTER 21: FOUR QUESTIONS MULTIFAMILY BROKERS HAVE WHEN QUALIFYING INVESTORS

"It's going to take time" – Kurt Shoemaker

Best Ever Guest: Kurt Shoemaker

Kurt Shoemaker is a Vice President at CBRE and a former Associate Vice President at Cassidy Turley based in Cincinnati, OH. In 2014, he was recognized as the Cassidy Turley Rising Star.

Episode 66

https://www.linkedin.com/in/kurt-shoemaker-5834839

Kurt got started in real estate after graduating from the University of Cincinnati with a finance degree. He became interested in the real estate industry as mainly because of his brother, who was working with Marcus and Millichap in Chicago. Unfortunately, Kurt entered the real world in 2008, when the market was going down big time and not many people were hiring. He was looking for a job that had a salary and to get his foot in the door so he could start learning the business, while making enough money to get by. Kurt took a job at Fidelity but quickly realized he did not want to be in that type of industry. He knew that Marcus and Millichap were hiring, but it was a 100% commission-based job. Kurt figured he was young so he might as well take the risk and just go for it.

Kurt quit his job at Fidelity and joined Marcus and Millichap, taking the 100% commission-based job. He decided to live at home, so he didn't have a mortgage or rent payment to deal with, which was very helpful. Kurt decided to focus on multifamily at a time when the market was not doing very well and not many deals were getting done. Most people might have thought it was a very bad time to get into the multifamily real estate business, but Kurt looked at it as an opportunity to get in while people were not working as hard and were falling out of the business. With this attitude, he was able to develop relationships and get some deals done, even in a very bad market.

Kurt was rocking and rolling at Marcus and Millichap and really wasn't looking to make a change anytime soon. After about 4 years, he was contacted by Cassidy Turley to see if he was interested in teaming up with a senior agent to help head up their multifamily division in Ohio, Kentucky, and Indiana. Kurt took the job with Cassidy Turley. In 2014, he was recognized as a Cassidy Turley Rising Star after closing on $55 million in multifamily deals.

Long-Term Approach

Kurt's mentors, including his brother who got him into the business, taught him that real estate is a long-term business. With all the different aspects of a deal, from financing to timing and everything in general, he knew it was going to take some time before he began seeing big results. Kurt tried to focus on not getting bogged down with the day-to-day struggle, although at times, he was asking himself "is making all these calls and putting in this work going to pay off?" In due time, it did. Looking back on his relatively short career, deals finally starting to come back around that he had worked on when he first started over six years ago. There were a couple that did hit early on, which allowed him to earn enough commission to get by.

In Kurt's six years in the real estate industry, he has seen many people come and go, including both brokers and investors. They come in wanting to close on a bunch of deals right away and make a lot of noise, but they fail to realize that it is not going to happen overnight. Kurt has met with many successful brokers who had been at it for years. They all say that the first four to five years were extremely challenging but by putting in the daily effort, all of the hard work paid off and they continue to reap the rewards today.

Advice in Action #1: Many people get confused when they think they will make a bunch of money and be successful immediately. In reality, it is going to take time and you will not see the results overnight. You need to have the mindset that the hard work will pay off as long as you consistently put in the time and effort.

Kurt does not own real estate currently, but would like to. When he does decide to start investing, he will adopt the same long-term approach he has as a broker. In this business, you look at deal after deal after deal. As a result, the ability to be patient and wait for the right deal can be very challenging. This is because you really want to get the ball rolling and put your money to work. Real estate investing can make you hundreds of millions of dollars, but it only takes one bad deal to kill your business plan. The right deal will come, but it is going to take time so you have to be willing to wait for the right fit. Don't jump on the wrong deal because you are impatient. Make sure that it fits everything you are looking for and if you have other investors, what they are looking for as well.

Advice in Action #2: Obviously, if you are not in the market taking action, you cannot expect a deal to just fall into your lap. You need to grow a large network of banks, brokers, financial advisors, accountants, etc., so that when a deal comes across their desk, you are the person they call. Off-market deals are great investment opportunities because you do not have to worry about competition as much. Get out there and grow a large network within the real estate

community so that when the time is right, you get the call and have a shot at the deal.

Qualifying a Deal

When qualifying someone as a serious investor for a deal, Kurt has four main questions:

1. *Can you show proof of funds?*

2. *What is your real estate background?*

3. *What real estate do you currently own?*

4. *What are you looking to buy?*

5. *The answers to all four of these questions determine if you qualify, and if so, what type of financing you can obtain.*

Just because you are able to qualify and obtain financing does not automatically mean you have a good deal. Kurt advises investors to have their underwriting criteria set before deciding to move forward with a deal. You must stay disciplined in only purchasing deals that meet your criteria.

Advice in Action #3: The types of underwriting criteria you need to set before going into a deal include:

- **Cap Rate**
- **Cash-on-Cash Return**
- **Exit strategies**
- **Estimated hold period**
- **Property type/strategy: distressed value-added, class A, or somewhere in-between**

Figure out what type of deal you need to buy in order to reach your goal, and stay disciplined!

Wrapping up Part Five

In Part Five, you received Best Ever Advice from two successful lenders.

In Part Six, you will receive Best Ever Advice from eight successful real estate professionals, as well as action items you can immediately implement in any real estate investment business. To begin, you will get the Best Ever Advice from a real estate lawyer on:

1. How to structure joint ventures so you're covered if the partnership breaks down

PART SIX:

THE BEST OVERALL REAL ESTATE INVESTING ADVICE EVER

CHAPTER 22: STRUCTURING JOINT VENTURES CORRECTLY

"Every day I'm hustlin'" – Rick Ross

Best Ever Guest: Ed Cox

Ed Cox owns Cox Law Firm PLLC, a Texas law firm devoted primarily to real estate and construction matters. He has practiced law for 19 years and has received Martindale-Hubbell's AV Preeminent rating, which is the highest rating for legal ability and ethical standards. Ed has also been selected a "Super Lawyer" and recognized as a "Top Attorney" in Texas Monthly.

Episode 20

http://www.edcoxlaw.com

Ed got into real estate when he took a job as a laborer in the construction industry in Texas when he was in 8th grade. He worked with his twin brother framing houses through high school. Ed also played piano growing up and wanted to be a professional musician. After high school, he attended Berkley College of Music in Boston to pursue this dream. However, he left after a year when he realized how difficult it would be to make a living as a professional piano player. Ed returned to Texas and graduated from the University of North Texas, where he received his degree in Political Science with a minor in Music.

In order to pay for school, Ed worked for several law firms in the Dallas Fort-Worth area serving subpoenas and citations. During this period, he met and learned from a several lawyers who interested him about the possibility of making law a career, so he decided to apply to law school. He was accepted into South Texas College of Law in Houston, Texas, and graduated with a law degree in 1995. Ed stayed in Houston until 2000, when he moved back to DFW to work for a law firm that focused on construction law. In 2002, Ed started a law firm with two other lawyers. Their firm opened a fee office for First American Title Company and began closing commercial and residential real estate transactions in 2003. In 2009, Ed formed his own law firm, Cox Law Firm, PLLC. A substantial portion of the firm's legal work is devoted to residential and commercial real estate and construction, as well as business litigation and transactions. In addition to practicing law, Ed continues to hold his escrow officer's license and now operates a fee office for Chicago Title.

Ed has handled a wide range of real estate matters, including the negotiation of purchase and sale contracts for various commercial and residential transactions, lawsuits involving real estate fraud, partnership disputes involving real estate transactions, trespass, eviction, and other claims. Ed has assisted clients with entitlements, zoning issues, and other disputes with municipalities. Ed also has experience litigating and arbitrating various commercial and residential construction claims and other civil matters.

Choose Wisely

As a lawyer with over 19 years of experience, Ed has a behind the scenes perspective on the majority of issues that real estate investors face during their careers and what you need to do in order to avoid them. Ed's best advice ever is to "choose wisely." He sees many people getting into partnerships, transactions, and business endeavors without actually consulting with people that have experience in similar business endeavors or neglecting to fully understand what they are getting into. Ed says that it is important to appreciate not only the potential benefits of the proposed transaction but also the potential risks and drawbacks.

Advice in Action #1: On the front end of undertaking a business endeavor with a partner or making any important business decision, it is important to understand the potential benefits AND potential risks or drawbacks. Sit down by yourself or with your business partner up-front, and perform the following exercise:

- **Brainstorm and list out benefits or rewards and potential risks or drawbacks that apply to your business situation.**

- **Compare and weigh the pros and cons against each other.**

- **Based on this comparison, make an educated decision on whether or not it makes sense to move forward.**

In the following sections, there are two examples of situations that serve as lessons on the potential consequences of failing to "choose wisely."

A Lesson in Partnerships and Due Diligence

The first example is a common situation that Ed faces. Many people come into his office, claiming to have been best friends for many years, and want to go into business together as 50/50 partners. He explains to them that if an issue arises and there is a disagreement between the two best friends, they could face a deadlock situation. Since the business is set-up as a 50/50 partnership, there may not be a viable way to resolve the disputes that may arise. On several occasions, Ed has seen best friends turn against each other in business endeavors and end up with problems that they never anticipated.

Advice in Action #2: The following are a few suggestions that Ed provided on how to avoid deadlock situations when going into a business as 50/50 partners:

- Find a 3rd party that has no vested interest in your business endeavor.

- Hammer out a specific dispute resolution procedure in the bylaws or your company agreement.

You need to understand that even with best friends, when people go into business or interact in general, disputes and disagreements will arise. It doesn't mean that anybody is necessarily right or wrong; it's just that people will inevitably have differences of opinions. Therefore, you really need to address this possibility upfront.

The second example is when Ed had a client who chose to buy a property at a foreclosure auction on the courthouse steps. Before purchasing, he drove by the house, but never made an effort to ascertain whether or not the property was vacant or occupied. It turned out the property was occupied, so after he bought the house, it took him 10 months to actually get the property in his possession and out of the hands of the current occupant. The occupant hired a lawyer and filed three different lawsuits against his client in three different courts. For Ed, this experience raised some novel and unique issues on dealing with evictions, but it was a very time consuming and expensive endeavor for his client. Ed and his client ultimately prevailed, but his client's expenditure of a large amount of money on the litigation was never a part of his investment game plan when he went to the courthouse steps 10 months earlier.

Advice in Action #3: Before purchasing a property at a foreclosure auction, make sure that you figure out the occupancy status of the property. Drive by the property and look for signs of vacancy.

Overgrown grass, overflowing mailbox, no trash cans at the end of the drive way on trash day, etc.

- Look for vehicles in the driveway or in front of the house

- **Drive by the property at night to see if any of the outside or inside lights are on**

- **Talk with neighbors to see if someone lives in the property**

Both of these examples, as well as most other issues real estate investors face, could have been prevented by following this piece of advice from Ed: think long and hard about what you are going to undertake, and try to assess and plan for any potential issues that may arise.

Advice in Action #4: In order to create a plan of action for potential issues that may develop, sit down alone or with your business partner, and using the list of risks or drawbacks from Advice in Action #1, perform the following exercise for each item:

- **Create a detailed step-by-step process on how you will handle this issue if it were to arise.**

- **Use each of these processes to create "dispute resolution procedures," and incorporate them into the bylaws or your company agreement.**

- **As disputes and disagreements arise, utilize the "dispute resolution procedures" you have agreed upon to try and resolve them without having your business fall apart or sit in an unproductive and protracted gridlock.**

In the next chapter, you will get the Best Ever Advice from a commercial real estate investor on:

1. How to identify and take advantage of an opportunity in the market that other investors dismiss

CHAPTER 23: DON'T FOLLOW THE HERD

"Buy when everyone else is selling" – *Warren Buffett*

Best Ever Guest: Arndt Nicklisch

Arndt Nicklisch is the founder of American Eagle Capital Partners. He is focused on investing in suburban office real estate.

Episode 28

http://www.aecp.com

Arndt got his start in real estate right after college, when he took a project management position on a construction site. He quickly realized that the people making all the money were developers and investors, not the people who were managing the sites. Therefore, he decided that he wanted in. Arndt went back to school and obtained his MBA from Harvard. After business school, he worked as a developer for a number of years and eventually was offered a position at the investment firm Colony Capital. At Colony Capital, Arndt joined a newly created platform called Colony Realty Partners, where he made investments in office, industrial, multifamily, and retail in almost every major market across the United States. That allowed him to see different cities, most property types, and all of the points on the risk spectrum.

Over the years, Arndt had seen many opportunities in the real estate market that no one seemed to be taking advantage of. This is where the idea for American Eagle Capital Partners was born. The company's mission would be to take advantage of the opportunities that others, including his current employer, were not. In 2014, Arndt founded American Eagle Capital Partners, which focuses on institutional quality assets that are temporarily out of favor or overlooked by other institutional investors. At this point in time, suburban office space was a dirty word among other investors. As a result, many investors were dismissing suburban office space, while Arndt and his new company took the time to take a closer look.

A Closer Look at a "Dirty Word"

After taking a closer look at suburban office space, Arndt discovered that the majority of people's jobs and homes were not near the stereotypical office buildings (high rises in the middle of the city or mixed development building with office, retail, and/or apartments) like downtown Manhattan. Instead, they were located outside of the downtown area. As a result, he figured there must be a demand for office space in these outside, suburban areas. At the time, the market was still recovering from the downturn, so the demand was not growing as quickly as it was in the heart of the city. However, Arndt believed that as the market recovered, this demand wouldn't disappear and would continue to grow.

Based on these findings, Arndt found benefits in three main areas: 1) competition, 2) demographics, and 3) costs.

1. Less Competition

With suburban office space being a dirty word, investors did not want to buy, and owners really wanted to sell. As a result, there was an oversupply in the market, which led to lower prices. There was also very little new construction occurring for these types of buildings. In a market as competitive as office space, this type of oversupply combined with a small number of buyers, highly motivated sellers, and a lack of new construction is very rare.

2. Demographics

Arndt and his company's focus is primarily on the younger demographic. These are people under the age of 35, and include singles, couples that have not started a family, or families with very young children. This is the same demographic that is being targeted on the residential and rental side. The idea behind this younger demographic is that as they mature in their situation in life, they will still want to move out to the suburbs. They are just making this move a little later in life compared to past generations. Single-family residences with a good yard and a good school are still appealing, and these types of benefits are typically found outside of the city in the suburbs. When they eventually move to these locations, the desire for a shorter commute arises, which makes these types of suburban office locations more favorable than a lengthy commute to the city.

3. Costs

Finally, Arndt believes there are huge cost advantages to these types of suburban office spaces. Rents are typically a fraction of what they typically are in a downtown high rise. Additionally, due to the benefits outlined in Less Competition, Arndt is able to purchase these properties below market value, which results in cost savings as well as higher profits.

Advice in Action #1: Arndt was able to identify and take advantage of an opportunity in the market that other investors dismissed, suburban office space. Take a deep dive into these three areas: competition, demographics, and costs. Depending on your current situation, this deep dive can aid in the following:

- **If you have already identified a niche, the results for this deep dive can confirm that your niche choice will be successful or it will tell you to avoid this altogether.**

- **If you are undecided, this deep dive can help you make a decision either way.**

- If you are just getting started, this can help you identify what niche to pursue.

Regardless of your situation, understanding the competition, demographics, and costs for a certain niche will help you unlock opportunities that others are not taking advantage of.

Advice in Action #2: Below are some questions you should be answering for your specific niche in the market:

- **Competition**
    - Is it a seller's or a buyer's market?
    - Who are the buyers?
    - Who are the sellers?
    - Is there new construction?
- **Demographics**
    - Who is the target demographic in regards age, income, family type, marital status, etc.?
    - Where are they living?
    - Where are they moving?
    - Where do they work?
    - How long is their commute?
    - Are they driving or using public transportation?
- **Costs**
    - Are properties being sold at a discount, at market value, or above market value?
    - What are the rents?
    - How do the rents of similar niches compare relative to average acquisition prices?

These are just a few examples of questions you need to be answering, but you should address additional questions based on the specific niche. **Most of this data can be found using online resources like Census.gov and city, country, or township websites.**

Don't Follow the Herd

With other investors dismissing suburban office space just because it was known as a dirty word, Arndt decided not to follow the herd and instead, form his own path. There are numerous situations where people are going to tell you "don't do this" and "only do that." By following this advice or giving out this advice yourself, you will miss out on some great opportunities. Throughout his 15 years of active real estate experience, Arndt has seen that the people who make it big are the ones who do not listen to the talking heads on TV or the negative advice from others. They are the ones who identify an opportunity in the marketplace, get really good at it, and present it to other people. As a result, all parties involved will benefit.

Advice in Action #3: It is important to get advice from others, but commit to investigating on your own by following the Advice in Action #1 and #2. This will help you determine for yourself whether it is good advice or bad advice.

By not following the herd, Arndt was able to create a great business that is very successful at investing in these suburban office spaces. In doing so, he has inherited valuable advice on how to thrive once you have identified an opportunity in the marketplace. Inside the suburban office space niche, Arndt and his company capture the full spectrum of property conditions. He has found success in value-added opportunities, which are properties that are under-leased, under-managed, or have not been upgraded in a long time. This includes anything that shows the property does not adhere to the current market requirements. Arndt also sees opportunities where all of the work has already been performed and the current cash flow yield of the building is attractive enough to justify their buy and hold strategy.

Advice in Action #4: Properties are typically under-leased or under-managed due to poor property management being in place. When deciding whether to take on the property management for yourself or to hire a better management company, Arndt believes it is important to outsource leasing and property management, especially for these larger assets. Find and hire the best property management company in your niche so you do not burden your investors or yourself with supporting the overhead for an in-house team.

Advice in Action #5: A technique that Arndt uses to help identify the potential value of a property is to see how the current owner is offering deals to prospective tenants. If the owner is offering deals (discounted rents, first month free, etc.), it can point to a whole slew of things.

In the next chapter, you will get two pieces of Best Ever Advice from a wholesaler on:

1. A step-by-step process for how to successfully wholesale probate properties

2. Why you need to create a marketing plan, stick to it, and never give up

CHAPTER 24: CRASH COURSE ON PROBATE WHOLESALING

"Be willing to live a few years how most people won't, so that you can live the rest of your life how most people can't" – Mastin Kipp

Best Ever Guest: Sharon Vornholt

Sharon Vornholt is a full-time real estate investor who focuses on wholesaling. She owned and operated a home inspection business for 17 years. She is also the host of the popular podcast "Let's Talk Real Estate Investing."

Episode 35

http://www.louisvillegalsrealestateblog.com

Sharon got started in real estate when she opened a home inspection business in 1991. In 1998, she went to the local REIA meetings and was instantly hooked. Sharon invested part-time, focusing on buy-and-holds and rehabs, while continuing to operate her home inspection business. In 2008, Sharon decided to close her home inspection business in order to focus on investing full-time as a wholesaler. She is actually an accidental wholesaler because it was not what she initially planned on pursuing. One of the niches that Sharon works in is probate. Sharon loves the probate niche because she discovered that when people inherit a property, they almost never want to keep the house and are among the most motivated sellers on the planet.

What is Probate?

According to Wikipedia, "the receipt of probate is the first step in the legal process of administering the *estate* of a deceased person resolving all claims and distributing the deceased person's property under a will. There are two types of probate processes, depending on whether or not the deceased individual has named someone in their will:

1. *Individual named in the will*

    • Referred to as *testate*

    • The individual named in the will is called the *executor* and takes care of the estate

2. *No individual named in the will or there is no will*

    • Referred to as *intestate*   No will

    • The court decides who takes care of the estate

    • Relatives of the deceased will go to court and petition to be in charge of the estate

    • The individual appointed is called the *administrator*

Both the executor and the administrator are interchangeably called the personal representative.

Advice in Action #1: If no individual is named in the will or there is no will, the family of the deceased has to rely on the judgment of the court on who will ultimately be given responsibility for the estate. Depending on state law, there is a priority list of which relative will be appointed, and many times it is not the individual who should have been appointed. In order to avoid this difficult situation, if you own any real estate, you should have a will stating who gets the property.

Probate Listing Property Types

The types of properties that end up in probate vary from state-to-state. In Sharon's market, Kentucky, she has found that people who have huge estates have typically done some sort of estate planning, so these types of properties rarely end up in probate. Typically, medium priced properties between $50,000 and $300,000 fall into probate situations.

Probate listings fall into one of three categories:

1. *Nice houses*
   - End up going on the MLS
   - Typically purchased by retail buyers
2. *Houses that are in bad shape*
   - Haven't been updated in a while and will need some work
   - Typically purchased by investors
3. *Houses that sit somewhere in the middle*
   - Maybe for-sale-by-owner
   - Maybe put on the MLS
   - Maybe not sold at all

Most investors focus on the properties in category two. They throw in the towel early on when going after the "maybe" situations in category three because the process isn't as fast. Sharon thrives in the "maybe" category because she has a professional, persistent approach to closing these types of deals.

Finding Probate Leads

Sharon finds direct mail to be the best source of finding leads because it gives her the ability to narrowly focus on specific types of leads, in this case, probate leads. When working with probate leads, there are four pieces of information required:

1. *Name of the deceased*
2. *Address of the deceased*
3. *Name of the personal representative*
4. *Address of the personal representative*

There are over 3,300 counties in the United States, and every one has a different probate process. Therefore, detective work is required in order to find these four pieces of information. In some areas, they are published in the newspapers. In other areas, a list can be found online. There are also services that sell probate leads but Sharon recommends trying to find them for free.

Sometimes, Sharon will look up an address and see that it is for a nursing home, but that doesn't necessarily mean the person does not have property. Most investors won't pursue a lead if a nursing home address comes up, but that does not stop Sharon. She will go to the tax assessor's site, look up the person by name, and see if there are any properties listed under their name.

In some areas, you can find probate leads online. You can search for "probate in (insert county name)" on Google and find websites that list the executor's name and address as well as the deceased name. The only additional piece of information required is the address of the deceased, which can be found on the tax assessor's site.

Reaching Out To Probate Leads

When reaching out to probate leads, Sharon only uses professional, computer generated white letters inserted into a hand written white business envelope. She never uses post cards or yellow letters. Sharon hears people complaining all the time about how disrespected they feel when receiving a yellow letter or post card.

Advice in Action #2: People going through probate hate receiving a casual yellow letter or postcard. They usually have a mess on their hands, so if you are interested in pursuing the niche of probate, make sure you follow Sharon's professional method.

As stated earlier, Sharon thrives in the probate property types that sit in the middle, the "maybes." Below is an example of a conversation she would have when a "maybe" seller calls after receiving a mailer, where Sharon offered to buy their property for $50,000:

- *Seller: "I have already listed the property with a real estate agent."*

- *Sharon: "I think it is a good idea if they can sell to a retail buyer, but can you still provide me with information about the property."*

   o   Sharon asks for information about the property because she wants to get a feeling herself on whether or not the home will actually sell.

- *Seller: "Everything is solid. The property is in good condition and does not require a lot of repairs."*

- *Sharon: "Thank you for that information. Is it okay if I keep you on my list?"*

- *Seller: "Yes, you can keep me on your list."*

   o   Due to Sharon's professionalism and understanding, she finds that the seller always says yes

- *Sharon: "Thank you. I hope that your plan works out but in case you are unable to sell, I would like to be your plan B. Also, if you do sell, can you please give me a call? I will take you off my list, so I do not pester you."*
   기회니-

Advice in Action #3: This same conversation structure can be used for other types of leads, not just for probates (i.e. motivated seller, out-of-state owners, landlords, etc.):

- Be polite, professional, and understanding
- Ask open-ended questions to obtain information regarding their situation
- If they say no or are not interested, offer to be their plan B

Take the time to write out a script, use it when you are speaking with potential leads, and make ongoing revisions based on the results

In the example above, there is a better likelihood the property will sell on the MLS. However, when the market was tighter, Sharon found that 50-70% of people in these situations still had the property 12-18 months later. Continuing with the example above, the same seller calls Sharon back 12 months later:

- *Seller: "Hi. Do you remember speaking with me about a year ago regarding the property at 123 Main Street I received via probate? You offered me $60,000."*

- *Sharon: (pulls up this property on her probate leads list) "Yes, I remember, but the offer was $50,000."*

- *Seller: "Okay. I would like to take you up on your offer, if you are still interested."*

In probate, the seller almost never keeps the property. If they have not sold it after a year, they will be very motivated to sell. However, you do not know exactly when they will be ready. In some situations, they are ready to sell right way, while in others, they may not be mentally ready for over a year.

Advice in Action #4: If you are working in the probate niche, you have to realize that the seller has recently lost a loved one and are going through a very difficult time. When doing direct mail or conversing on the phone, you have to be careful. Use a helpful tone and acknowledge the fact that they may not be ready to sell right way. Let them know that you will be checking back in with them from time to time.

Don't Give Up On Your Marketing

Sharon's Best Ever on what separates investors who make it and the ones who don't is creating a marketing plan, sticking to it, and never giving up. This applies to wholesalers, buy-and-hold, fix-and-flip, and all other types of investors. You need to think of your marketing plan as a strategy that will work over time. Sharon sees investors who send out a couple pieces of mail over a period of 3 to 4 months, don't get a deal or the number of deals they were expecting, say marketing doesn't work, and then quit. She loves people like this because she continues to mail, and ends up being the last one standing.

With probates, Sharon deals with people who mentally cannot get the house cleaned out for over a year. Therefore, she ends up buying a lot of the properties around the one-year mark. The sellers tell her they received a bunch of letters for 3 to 4 months, but Sharon's letters are the only ones they receive now. By continuing to send out letters, Sharon's name is at the forefront of their minds, and due to her professionalism, they view her as a real business. Her letters are professional, acknowledge that she will be there when they are ready, and that she can help them with settling the estate. As a result, the seller feels like they have built a relationship with her, more so than with the investors who send the typical casual yellow letter or post card.

Advice in Action #5: You cannot give up just because you haven't gotten any results from a few months of marketing. Instead, commit to sending out mailers every 4 weeks. Sharon uses a series of about six different letters she cycles through. Continue mailing every four weeks until you either buy the property, or it is sold to someone else.

As you discover properties are sold or every four to six months, scrub your list and remove any properties that have already sold.

In the next chapter, you will get two pieces of Best Ever Advice on:

1. Why it's important to focus on where you're buying instead of what you're buying

2. How to determine when it's the right time to refinance a property

CHAPTER 25: BUY THE NEIGHBORHOOD, NOT THE HOUSE

"I just want to live happy." – Nela's child

Best Ever Guest: Nela Richardson

Nela Richardson is currently the Chief Economist for Redfin. She is a former John Hopkins University professor of Finance and a former researcher at Harvard. Nela has been an interview guest on CNN, Bloomberg TV, CSPAN, CBS Radio and more.

Episode 42

http://www.redfin.com

Nela got started in real estate over 10 years ago, when she took a job as a housing economist at Freddie Mac, one of the largest mortgage insurers in the country. At that point, it was a great time for the housing market. Credit was cheap, getting a mortgage was easy, and prices were booming, so there were many active investors in the market. As you know, all of that activity had a price, and the economy paid for it. The housing bubble burst and the economy went into a financial crisis in 2008.

As a result of the crisis, Nela transitioned to the regulation side of real estate. She did a stint at Harvard where she conducted research on the financial crisis to determine what events had led up to it. The goal of her research was to formulate regulations that would help contain the banks and investors, as well as homeowners, so this magnitude of crisis could never happen again to the real estate market. Nela's conclusion: tougher underwriting standards.

The government already had the power to impose and enforce regulations on how mortgages were supposed to be underwritten by banks. They just needed to actually enforce these existing regulations. Therefore, rules were put into place to help in this effort. All of the toxic mortgage products like negative amortization mortgages, interest only mortgages, and mortgages that required no documentation of income virtually disappeared. The remaining products were safer mortgages so most people could feel confident that the population would not go into default in mass, which is what happened when the housing bubble burst in 2008.

Lessons Learned From Financial Crisis

The years immediately following the financial crisis were very tight. Nela compares the real estate market to a pendulum that swings back and forth. Before the financial crisis, the pendulum had swung too far to the side of easy credit, which was not good. After the financial crisis, the pendulum swung too far to the side of very strict standards, which made it very difficult to get a mortgage. This was also no good. Due in part to the type of work that Nela did at Harvard, over time, banks became less conservative and started easing their standards to help the average person making an average salary obtain a mortgage. She believes that having the pendulum at a happy medium between the two extremes is crucial for the housing market to completely recover. This is great news for potential homebuyers moving forward.

In regards to the industries that have recovered the fastest, Nela has seen multifamily really shoot up and recover faster than single-family residences. There is a high demand for apartments, and builders quickly caught on to this fact. As a result, multifamily properties and apartments are being built at a much stronger rate than other types of properties.

This is great news for the rental side of the real estate industry. However, it leads to a lack of inventory on the homebuyer front, meaning there are fewer homes for sale.

Nela also sees a demand by the millennial population. The millennial population, ages 25 to 34, is the largest part of the population coming to the market needing a place to live. It has been said that the millennial population has been living in their parent's basements waiting for jobs, but they are not going to stay there forever. As they begin to move out, they are not going to be purchasing a single-family residence in the suburbs. Instead, they are likely going to move into an apartment, so that is a good business to be in right now.

Advice in Action #1: Nela believes multifamily rental properties and apartments have the highest demand in the post financial crisis real estate market, specifically for the millennial generation. Take a look at your target market to see if this is the case and if it is something you should consider as your investment strategy moving forward.

Buy the Neighborhood

For potential homebuyers, Nela believes it is very important to buy the neighborhood, not just the house. This is especially true after researching the causes and effects of the financial crisis. People get caught up in the details of the house, square footage, kitchen, master bath, etc., and end up losing sight of where the house is actually located. At the end of the day, the neighborhood will have a larger effect on appreciation over time than the house itself. You can buy a great house in a bad neighborhood, but you will not see the level of recovery or surge in price that you might see in a similar house in a different neighborhood.

Advice in Action #2: Follow Nela's advice and focus more on where you are buying, and not what you are buying. We have all heard the

saying "location, location, location," so it is important for your business that you commit to always adhering to this advice.

When to Refinance

In regards to refinancing, Nela advises to only do so when it makes sense. Many people will get a 30-year fixed rate mortgage and then never think about it again. Interest rates for mortgage loans fluctuate over time. They will continually go up and down, so the best time to refinance is when these rates are down. Therefore, it is important to understand and recognize when the rates are historically low, so you can take advantage and lock in a lower rate.

Advice in Action #3: Nela is surprised by how slow mortgage rates have increased given all the things the Federal Reserve has been doing differently, but she still believes it will be a few years until we see a big bump up in rates. A rate around 5% is still a great rate when you consider that rates were 10-12% 20 years ago. You may have missed the lowest rates, but you are still in a good position. Take a look at your current portfolio to see if it makes sense to refinance into a lower rate.

Another situation where it makes sense to refinance is when you have paid down your loan or your property value has increased to the point that you have 20% or more equity. Once you hit this 20% mark, you are able to eliminate private mortgage insurance (PMI), which will decrease your monthly mortgage payment.

Advice in Action #4: If you are not comfortable refinancing because you do not want the 30-year clock to start over again, another option that might make sense is to refinance into a 15-year mortgage, depending on how high your current rate is and/or how low the market rates are. For example, if you take a 30-year fixed 6% interest conventional loan and compare it with a 15-year fixed 3% interest rate

conventional loan, the monthly payments are virtually the same. The biggest difference is that with a 15-year loan, you are paying off your mortgage 15 years faster.

There are many other ways for buyers and investors to lower their mortgage payments, so it is important to be knowledgeable on the full range of mortgage options when making a mortgage related decision.

In the next chapter, you will get two pieces of Best Ever Advice on:

1. Why it is important to build a solid foundation of knowledge before jumping into real estate

2. How to build trusting relationships with local real estate professionals using a different kind of due diligence

CHAPTER 26: A DIFFERENT KIND OF DUE DILIGENCE

"It's impossible" said pride, "it's risky" said experience, "it's pointless" said reason, "give it a try" said the heart - Unknown

Best Ever Guest: Engelo Rumora

Engelo Rumora is the CEO and Founder of Ohio Cash Flow. He is originally from Australia, and now invests strictly in the United States.

Episode 52

http://www.engelorumora.com

Engelo got his start in real estate when he began working as a laborer on dirty construction sites in Australia. He was fortunate enough to receive a book from one of his work colleagues, "Rich Dad, Poor Dad" by Robert Kiyosaki, which completely hooked him on real estate. As a result, Engelo started focusing more on learning about business and finance so he could find a better way of making a living than being a laborer. He began attending many personal development seminars, reading books, going to different real estate events, meeting with high net worth individuals and asking a lot of questions, and just learning as much as he could about real estate. Through this education process, Engelo was able to get a job with one of the most successful real estate professionals in all of Australia. He worked as a buyer's agent and seller's agent, negotiated on deals, and did anything and everything on a daily basis.

After working side-by-side with this professional for about a year and a half, Engelo combined everything he had learned with the construction knowledge he gained working as a laborer, and purchased his first deal. At the time, Engelo only had $40,000 to his name, but because of his years of hands-on real estate training, he was able to purchase 7 additional properties over the next 6 months. The key to scaling quickly was due to his creative 4-step business model:

1. *Purchase distressed properties below market value.*

2. *Renovate the property (due to his construction background, he was able to perform most of the renovations).*

3. *Knock on the bank's door and ask for an 80% LTV refinancing.*

4. *The refinancing would give him a cash injection of $40,000 to $50,000 and he would repeat the process.*

In the US, it is difficult to find a bank to refinance an investment property. However, it is a completely different world in Australia. In Australia, there are only five major banks that finance residential or investment loans. When Engelo was maxed out at one lender, he would just go to another bank and see if they would be willing to financing any more properties. Going from one lender to another enabled Engelo to build a large portfolio in a short time frame.

Advice in Action #1: Instead of just jumping into real estate, Engelo took that time, over one and a half years, to educate himself on all facets of the real estate business. You do not have to spend a year and a half on education like Engelo, but it is important to build a solid foundation of knowledge so you can avoid making the simple mistakes.

Australia Flips to US Buy and Holds

Even though Engelo was having considerable success following his 4-step process, he realized that it was not a sustainable investing model. He saw that he was overleveraged and was basing his analysis on predictions that the property was going to go up in value more than on what he would lose on a monthly basis in holding costs. After this realization, Engelo decided to begin looking for properties that provided more cash flow. Unfortunately, these types of cash flowing properties were not available in Australia. However, he discovered there were many more cash flow opportunities in the United States.

The first property that Engelo purchased outside of Australia was a C-class single-family in Kansas City. He purchased the property for $11,000, put in an additional $10,000 in renovations, and rented it out for $600 a month. All said and done, the property had a 25-30% cap rate, and Engelo believes this is probably one of the best investments he has ever made. After seeing how attractive the returns were in the United States, he immediately began selling all of his properties in Australia and moved all of his capital to the US market, purchasing another property in Upstate New York.

Engelo is currently focused on purchasing distressed, run down single-family properties in the Ohio market, fixing them up, getting them rented out, and either selling to investors or adding them to his buy-and-hold portfolio. He is looking more into commercial and multifamily deals because he is seeing numerous great opportunities to get bigger returns with the same amount of effort.

Focus on Trust and Relationships

The first item on the agenda for Engelo after he decided to invest in the United States was to establish the right connections on the ground. After initially selecting the Kansas City market, he focused on locating and conducting due diligence on potential team members before making the decision to invest in the market. He advises everyone to focus on building trusting relationships rather than focusing on the stats and demographics of the particular area. Once you have established the right connections, you can actually start looking at the data.

Advice in Action #2: Whether you are investing out of the state, out of the country, or in your own backyard, focus on building trusting relationships with local real estate professionals first. These professionals should be:

- **Realtors**
- **Rehabbers**
- **Property Managers**
- **Attorneys**
- **Accountants**
- **Anyone else who you need to succeed in any particular market**

As investors, we often get caught up in finding the perfect market. However, if we don't find the right team members, then the market is of no value to us. On the flip side, if we have a market that is okay, but we have an amazing team, then there will always be opportunities in that market. For example, if you buy the best house on the best street with the best capital growth predications, but the people looking after your property are incompetent and cheaters, you are always going to lose money. By contrast, Engelo knows investors that are making millions of dollars in less than desirable areas of Detroit because the property managers are trustworthy, know what they are doing, understand the market, and pay out the investor. It comes down to really establishing the trusting relationships with people who are loyal, honest, and not greedy. If you have this, the sky is the limit.

Advice in Action #3: After locating your team members, create a due diligence process in order to determine if they are the right fit for

what you are looking to do. Brainstorm a list of questions you can ask potential team members see if they:

- Are trustworthy
- Know what they are doing
- Know the market
- Are loyal, honest, not greedy, etc.

You want to screen potential team members the same way you would screen potential tenants. There is information and action items in other chapters that can help you learn how to conduct your due diligence. However, some tips for getting good answers include:

- Talk to references
- Visit past projects
- Ask them for an example of a business relationship that didn't go well. If they do not have any examples of a business relationship that didn't go well, then they either haven't been in the business long enough or they aren't being truthful – both of which are disqualifiers in my book.

In the next chapter, you will get the Best Ever Advice on:

1. Why you don't invested based on unfounded optimism and emotions

CHAPTER 27: DON'T INVEST ON UNFOUNDED OPTIMISM AND EMOTIONS

"Luck is when opportunity meets preparation." - Seneca

Best Ever Guest: Theresa Bradley-Banta

Theresa Bradley-Banta is the founder and CEO of Theresa Bradley-Banta Real Estate Consultancy, which has won 11 American and International real estate rewards. She is the author of "Invest in Apartment Buildings: Profit without the Pitfalls." Theresa is also the 2012 winner of the Stevie Award for Entrepreneur of the Year.

Episode 68

http://www.theresabradleybanta.com

Theresa got started in real estate in 2004 by purchasing and managing rental properties. In 2005, she attended a national wealth-building seminar with her husband and decided to add passive real estate investing to her portfolio. At this seminar, they came across two investment groups whose services they ended up utilizing for their first out-of-state investments. These investment groups identified properties in Ohio and New York, purchased them using Theresa's funds, and then conducted a majority of the work (renovations and management), making for strictly passive investing.

Theresa's experiences working with these investment groups shed some light on two issues. First, the difficulties faced when investing out-of-state. Secondly, as a passive investor, Theresa did not have a lot of say in what was happening. The combination of these two issues led her to decide to invest in her own backyard, working primarily as a renovator and flipper of residential real estate.

Over the last 12 years, Theresa has been involved in many aspects of the real estate business. She has flipped properties from $50,000 to $2.5 million across the nation. She founded Theresa Bradley-Banta Real Estate Consultancy, which has won 11 American and International Real Estate Rewards. Theresa is the author of "Invest in Apartment Buildings: Profit without the Pitfalls." In 2006, Theresa was involved in her first out-of-country business endeavor in the capacity of an investor and advisory group founder for a development deal in Mexico.

Mexico Development

The Mexico deal was a residential development project outside of a resort area. The project involved developing the land into lots that were used for building residential residences for either vacation homes or people's second homes. This deal came about during an annual wealth-building seminar that she attended in Mexico. During this seminar, members of the wealth-building group tossed around the idea of a development project over margaritas. One of the members at the table had built a home in Mexico and lived there for half the year and another woman knew someone who was currently doing developments in the area. Due to the experienced members at the table, they decided to move forward with the project.

Theresa was able to get in on the ground floor by leading the advisory group that oversaw the covenants and restrictions for the development, which will eventually be the Home Ownership Association (HOA). Up to this point, HOAs had been a pain during the other investments that Theresa had done, so being on the other side was a very illuminating experience.

There are international challenges that make ownership in Mexico different than ownership in the United States, so the education piece on what is or isn't allowed is very important. Since she had met so many good people that knew the Mexico laws, had already developed real estate in Mexico, and had experience living in both the United States and Mexico, Theresa had a team with the education and experience that gave her the confidence to move forward with this deal.

Don't Invest on Unfounded Optimism and Emotions

Theresa was obviously excited about the prospect of investing in Mexico, but she made sure that she did her due diligence and was surrounded with an experienced team before making the decision to move forward. She did not invest based on her excitement alone because Theresa's best advice is to "never invest on unfounded optimism and emotions."

For example, let's say you find a deal on a 2-bedroom rental where the numbers look great and you really want to close on the property. Your real estate agent advises against the purchase because 4-bedroom rentals are in demand in this market, not 2-bedroom rentals. You erroneously believe that the property is in demand and respond by saying "I am optimistic things will change. I am optimistic it will be better." Theresa thinks this is a huge mistake.

Advice in Action #1: Don't invest on unfounded optimism. Just because the numbers make sense, does not mean the deal automatically makes sense. Be patient, perform your due diligence, and make an educated decision on whether or not to move forward.

Another example is when people fall in love with a property or have an emotional attachment to a property. Theresa was looking at a building on the East Coast with a client that was the coolest building. It was an old school house that was converted into apartments and had a "cool factor" because of the layout, space, staircases, foyers, etc. The numbers were solid, and the current owner said nearby schools would provide perfect potential tenants. However, tenants with numerous collection issues and late payments currently occupied the property.

At this point, Theresa's client was in love with the property and was enthusiastic on making an offer, but Theresa took a step back, and went to the local police to get a police report. The police stated that the tenants in that market will likely never change, at least not in the next five to ten years, making it a very high risk deal to do.

It is easy to say that a property is so cool that you can just picture the right tenants in there. If you only go on this optimistic assumption, when you are the owner, you will find that you can't easily change that market. From Theresa's experiences, she finds that it might take 5-10 years before you see any significant changes, so the tenants who were living there when you closed the deal will be type of tenant you find in that market for quite a while. As a result, you will have some serious problems on your hands.

Advice in Action #2: You can only reposition a property so much. There a certain things you can change about real estate, but location is not one of them. If you purchase a property with the optimism that you will somehow be able to change the market, you will run into some serious issues.

There are times you can influence the direction of a neighborhood through community service efforts, getting involved in local government or other methods, but it's an uphill battle. If you decide to do that, then I commend you for taking that approach, but I don't recommend running your numbers assuming it will turn around.

In the next chapter, you will get the Best Ever Advice on:

1. How to build a luxury brand on a shoestring budget

CHAPTER 28: BUILDING A LUXURY BRAND ON A SHOESTRING BUDGET

"Live well, laugh often, love much." – Bessie Anderson Stanley

Best Ever Guest: Madison Hildebrand

Madison Hildebrand is a founding partner of Partners Trust's Malibu Office, a Beverly Hills based brokerage with approximately 200 agents. He formerly co-starred in Bravo's hit series Million Dollar Listing Los Angeles. Madison is the author of "Activate YOUR Passion, Create YOUR Career" and has his own scented candle collection called The Malibu Life by Madison Hildebrand.

Episode 78

http://www.themalibulife.com

Madison got started in real estate over ten years ago in the 90265 zip code of Malibu, California. For him, it was really about building a perception of luxury, which is what he wanted to make his brand feel and look like. Madison wanted to be perceived as luxury.

Madison went to Pepperdine University, where he studied advertising and marketing. When he was 26, he obtained his real estate license. He did not have any prior real estate experience but it was something he became very passionate about. His brand and perception was about really connecting with people and making it about service, because that is what Madison believes gives him the ability to create the most value.

Building A Luxury Brand on a Shoestring Budget

When you think about luxury, the first thing that comes to mind is usually money. At the time, Madison did not have a lot of money to his name, but through creativity and effort, he was able to attain the perception of luxury with a small budget. Madison believes that the best path to creating a luxury brand is through smart networking.

When Madison first got started, he made it a point to reach out to hotel general managers and concierges in the area. He would ask to make an appointment and then entertain them with half an hour of conversation. Madison did not have to take them out to a fancy lunch. He just wanted to get his face in front of these people who potentially have clients who are coming into town and may have an interest in staying longer than for just a short hotel visit. These meetings were his first free connections to potential clients.

Advice in Action #1: For Madison, reaching out to the hotel managers and concierges was a free way he could network and give him the opportunity to connect with potential clients. Who are people you can reach out to today that can do the same thing for you? Just like Madison, you do not have to take them to lunch, but simply entertaining them with a half hour of conversation over coffee will do the trick.

Another action Madison took when he first got started, was reaching out to the editors of articles of the LA Times, Forbes, and whoever wrote about real estate. Editors always post their contact information or social media accounts in their articles, so whenever Madison came across a real estate related article, he would reach out. Out of every ten attempts, he would get about one response. Madison's goal was to get the editors to use him as a quote, which would get his name in one of their articles. He would then recirculate the article to everyone within his sphere of influence. Madison was able to get quoted in a Forbes.com article within the first three months of being in business. Just by being able to say that he was quoted on Forbes.com carried a lot of clout, which he was able to use to further promote his own brand as being a credible source in the real estate industry.

Advice in Action #2: Just because you are a totally new investor, does not mean you can't follow in Madison's footsteps. He started reaching out to editors and was able to get quoted within the first three months of starting his business. When you come across a real estate article, which you should be reading anyway, take the time to reach out to the article's editor. Let them know you enjoyed the article and provide your personal insight on the article's topic.

As Madison's brand become more popular, he started getting invited to speak around the country on different real estate topics, like networking, luxury, and branding. He was even able to be on the reality TV, Million Dollar Listing on Bravo, for six years. This helped Madison create a large social media following, which he uses to share advice and details about his business as an outlet for free press.

Advice in Action #3: Everyone now uses some sort of social media platform nowadays. It is a great and easy way to build your brand and to show that you are the go to expert in your field. But don't try to do it all at once. Pick one social media platform and do it well.

In the next chapter, you will get two pieces of Best Ever Advice on:

1. Why you cannot underestimate the value of your brand
2. A step-by-step approach to building a powerhouse real estate brand

CHAPTER 29: CREATE A POWERHOUSE REAL ESTATE BRAND

"Be yourself; everyone else is already taken." – Oscar Wilde

Best Ever Guest: Herman Chan

Herman Chan was recognized in Klout's Top 50 Most Influential in Real Estate Investing. He has been featured on HGTV, CNN Money, CBS, CNBC, USA Today and House Hunters. Herman is also the author of "LOOKING UP: Images to Uplift."

Episode 89

http://www.habitatforhermanity.com

Herman was born and raised in the Bay Area and went to UC Berkley. As a result, he has a very big network in that area. After graduating, he was trying to figure out what he wanted to do in life. Herman's mother told him to get his real estate license to stay afloat financially while he tried to find himself. At this point, Herman felt lost. He was doing what everyone else was doing, trying to be laced up, serious, and professional, but this never really resonated with him. Herman was never talking about his personal life with work colleagues. He was just clocking in and clocking out and was never really connecting with people.

In order to fill this void, Herman decided to start a blog to just show a lighter side of real estate as well as his personality. All of a sudden, he was attracting people more like him, and was starting to build what business people call "brand loyalty." Herman's blog was resonating with his readers and attracted people who shared a similar worldview. This made him realize the importance of just being his authentic self, putting himself out there, taking an opinion and standing by it, and most importantly, that he cannot be everything to everyone.

In general, Herman believes just being your true self is the hardest thing in the world. There is so much puffery and fakery in the business world that it is very difficult to be your authentic self. Herman learned this lesson firsthand when he graduated from college and felt lost. Now, he believes if you want to live a happy and fulfilling life, you have to be comfortable being your authentic self, and building your brand around this notion.

Don't Underestimate the Value of Your Brand

Herman, personally, does not like the word "brand" because he says it sounds calculating and manipulative. When he is speaking to the broader public or potential clients, he does not claim himself as a brand and does not come off as self-righteous. That being said, Herman still knows that it is vital we do not underestimate the value of our brand. When you put something out on social media, the press, and how you present yourself are all extensions of who you are.

Herman's biggest lesson is that perception is reality. We live in a hyper social media and Internet world where everything is at the tip of people's fingertips. People do not really do a lot of research when they are trying to learn more about you or your brand. They just Google you and within the first couple of hits, they will form an opinion of you. They will look you up on Twitter, look at your last few posts and your 140-character bio and then judge you.

As an investor, you may think you are comfortable being on the sideline and staying anonymous, but that is not the world we live in. When people are doing deals with you, not just clients, but also all real estate professionals, they have access to everything about you. They can Google your LLC and trace it back to you in a matter of minutes. Herman believes that it is extremely important to manage your online reputation because it will make or break you. If someone can't find you, they think you do not exist, which makes them insecure about doing business with you.

Advice in Action #1: Whether you are just starting out or you are a veteran investor, you have to craft your message so succinctly and carefully that when people just Google your name, they can find you within the first 10 seconds.

Initially, with being on TV, Herman felt all high and mighty and thought people would just Google him and see how great he was. One time, he received a Google alert for a recent Yelp review. Herman thought it was going to be another 5 star review, but it ended up being a 1 star review. He was listing a property that had 16 offers, two-thirds being all cash. One couple that did not submit a cash offer posted a review claiming they were promised the property at an open house and that Herman double-ended (double-ended means dual agency: real estate agent represents both the buyer and the seller) it. Even though this was untrue, Herman realized that this 1 star review was out there for the whole world to see. His mistake was not being proactive and claiming the Yelp review account. Eventually, the review was flagged and removed. However, Herman realized that even someone who was out there as much as him still needed to be actively managing his or her online reputation.

Advice in Action #2: Proactively manage your online reputation. Anytime someone puts your name into Google, you want to control what pops up. It is just a numbers game. The more positive information you have out there, the better.

Practical Ways to Build Your Brand

Throughout his career, Herman has discovered practical ways to build a solid brand. One of the best ways to start is to Google your name to see what comes up. You can also set up a Google Alert so if someone writes about you, you are instantly notified. Because of the way Google and SEO works, you almost have to bury yourself and get ahead of people before they find you. You have to manage the conversation and put content out there all the time. This may seem difficult or tedious, but it is not as hard as the potential damage of someone posting something negative about you, or even worse, not having a presence at all. Another tool that Herman uses is Yelp. He has received countless leads from procuring free Yelp reviews. He also actively participates in blogs, responding on Trulia, and posting and responding on his own personal blog.

Advice in Action #3: Commit to taking action on at least one of the following practical ways Herman uses to build his brand:

- **Google your name to see what comes up**
- **Set up a Google Alert for your name**
- **Create a Yelp account**
- **Create and post to a Trulia, Zillow, or other online real estate platform**
- **Post to online real estate blogs**
- **Create and post to your own real estate blog**

Another technique you can use to build your brand is to create and utilize an Instagram account. We are becoming an increasingly visual culture. Ten years ago, blogs were the go to space. Then it was Facebook and Twitter. It is now Snapchat, Vine, and Instagram. Herman likes Instagram the most because you can use it to easily brand yourself without posting a lot and without a lot of work. You are creating a brand by association and you are creating your image by the images you take.

Advice in Action #4: Use Instagram and other similar social media platforms as a visual blog. Even if you have nothing to do with what you are posting, you can still talk about it. You want to create a storyline on your feed to position yourself as someone who is active and knows what is going on in the market. As people begin reaching out to you, start having conversations and tag back and forth. You will start to build a following and maybe even get a lead.

Social media in general, but especially visual social media, is all about being vetted. When you meet someone, they will look you up online. They want to work with someone they can trust and someone that is involved in the business. All aspects of your brand have to be seamless.

Advice in Action #5: The following are a few examples of how you can utilize visual social media to build your brand:

- **As a Real Estate Agent**
    - o Let's say you are a real estate agent who wants to sell Victorian homes
    - o Go out and take pictures of Victorians around your city. It does not matter if you sold them
    - o Your goal is to position yourself as a Victorian expert and this can be accomplished by simply posting about Victorians
    - o You can blast your feed across the Internet by simultaneously posting to Tumblr, Four Square, Twitter, and Facebook
    - o By consistently putting yourself out there, all of a sudden, you are known as the queen (or king) of Victorians
- **As a Fix and Flipper**
    - o If you fix and flip homes, post before and after pictures of your projects

- o Due to the allure of HGTV, everyone loves a good make over

- o Why wouldn't you want to post before and after pictures of your projects?

- o If you are not currently flipping a property, you can post images of past projects

- **As a Newer Investor**

  - o As a new investor, visual social media is the perfect way to have a blog that tracks your entire journey

  - o You can post about new information you have learned, images of properties you are viewing, and anything and everything else you are doing that is related to your progress towards purchasing your first property

  - o It is great to follow an investor that has done hundreds of flips or controls million of dollars in real estate, but as a brand new investor, you can connect with your followers on a more personal level because you have a lot more in common with them

CONCLUSION

So there you go. That's some of the Best Ever advice from the first 100 episodes of my podcast, The Best Real Estate Investing Advice Ever Show.

But guess what?

This advice isn't worth the paper it's printed on unless you implement it. That's why I challenge you to implement one piece of advice. That's right. You just got 29 chapters full of stories and ways to implement the lessons learned, but if you're like me, then you might be waiting until you finish the book to take action.

Well, now is the time. Take action.

Which story resonated with you most? And which piece of advice are you going to act on?

Let me know by posting at www.facebook.com/meetjoefairless/. I'll do what I can to support you with your endeavors and I look forward to hearing from you.

Get caught up on the latest Best Ever episode at www.joefairless.com.

Lastly, all profits from the sale of this book are being donated to Junior Achievement. Thank you for your support and please ask your friends, family, and colleagues to grab a copy so they get access to the Best Real Estate Investing Advice Ever while helping a great cause.

ACKNOWLEDGEMENTS

My family for your love and support throughout my entrepreneurial journey.

Colleen, the love of my life and the Chief Editor of this book.

My co-author, Theo Hicks. AKA, The Brain. You have a talent for breaking down large amounts of information into easily understandable and actionable insights

My investors. Without your belief in my business model of buying apartment and sharing in the profits, this book wouldn't have been possible.

Lauren Dinkens who was instrumental in the strategic development of this book.

And, of course, all the loyal Best Ever Listeners.

ABOUT THE AUTHORS

Joe Fairless

From being the youngest vice president of a New York City ad agency to creating a company that in 6 months controlled over $7,000,000 of property, Joe Fairless lives up to his Fearless Fairless nickname.

He's the host of the popular podcast, Best Real Estate Investing Advice Ever show, which is the world's longest running daily real estate podcast. Past interview guests include Barbara Corcoran and Robert Kiyosaki.

He currently controls over $54,000,000 of real estate and consults investors who want to raise money and buy apartment buildings.

He currently resides in Cincinnati, Ohio and is on the Alumni Advisory Board for The College of Media and Communication at Texas Tech University and the Board of Directors for Junior Achievement.

Say hi to him at www.joefairless.com.

Theo Hicks

Theo Hicks went from graduating from The Ohio State University with a degree in chemical engineering in 2013 to purchasing his first multi-family property in February 2015, while having no previous experience in real estate investing whatsoever. Flashing forward to the present, he has quit his w2 job, obtained his real estate license, and has become a full-time real estate investor, author, and podcast host. He is 26 years old.

He is the co-author of the Best Ever Weekly Newsletter, which provides actionable tips, much like this book, from Joe's podcast on a weekly basis.

He is passionate about the psychological, personal development side of success. Therefore, he created the Unplugged Podcast where he shares his knowledge, experiences, insights, and opinions, as well as provides actionable advice, to help real estate investors, or any professional in general, have a better understanding of themselves and the human condition so that they can maximize their potential and create a truly fulfilling life!

He currently resides in Cincinnati, OH.

Listen to his most recent podcast episode and say hi to him at www.theohicks.org